Speaking of Teaching . . .

Speaking of Teaching . . .

Inclinations, Inspirations, and Innerworkings

Avraham Cohen
City University of Seattle, Canada

Marion Porath
The University of British Columbia, Canada

Anthony Clarke
The University of British Columbia, Canada

Heesoon Bai
Simon Fraser University, Canada

Carl Leggo
The University of British Columbia, Canada

Karen Meyer
The University of British Columbia, Canada

SENSE PUBLISHERS
ROTTERDAM/BOSTON/TAIPEI

A C.I.P. record for this book is available from the Library of Congress.

ISBN: 978-94-6091-785-1 (paperback)
ISBN: 978-94-6091-786-8 (hardback)
ISBN: 978-94-6091-787-5 (e-book)

Published by: Sense Publishers,
P.O. Box 21858,
3001 AW Rotterdam,
The Netherlands
https://www.sensepublishers.com/

Printed on acid-free paper

Cover art:
Porath, M. (2008). Lily [Wood engraving]. Vancouver, BC.

Closing art:
Porath, M. (2011). Variations on a lily [Wood engraving]. Vancouver, BC.

All Rights Reserved © 2012 Sense Publishers

No part of this work may be reproduced, stored in a retrieval system, or transmitted in any form or by any means, electronic, mechanical, photocopying, microfilming, recording or otherwise, without written permission from the Publisher, with the exception of any material supplied specifically for the purpose of being entered and executed on a computer system, for exclusive use by the purchaser of the work.

TO THE PEOPLE WHO MATTER TO US AS TEACHERS

My work in this book is dedicated to my teachers who were crucial to all I have become to this point in my life: To Dr. Peter Lavelle, who when I was 26 and just starting out in my professional life, saw much more in me than I had any clue about, and at an extremely challenging time in my life. To Dr. David Berg who showed me a different philosophy and way of seeing and living in the world. I was stupefied when he killed himself. Even then, he was still my teacher showing me that life is uncertain and that every moment is precious. To Heesoon, my on-site personal Zen master; no more needs to be said. To Aunt Evalyn, who died yesterday, August 14, 2011 at the age of 101. She always, always saw what was good in me. And to the Great Teacher that is the relational field of our group.

Avraham Cohen

To Mrs. Everall, my Grade six teacher, who noticed, encouraged, and allowed me to believe in my artistic self; Mr. Chave, my high school English teacher who did the same for my identities as writer and scholar; and Dr. Robbie Case, doctoral mentor and friend, who brought it all together. Robbie's elegant scholarship, wisdom, intellectual creativity, and commitment to a community of scholars were pivotal in shaping who I am today. Most specially to Merv for your support and belief in me—Your humour, balance, and strength allow me to be.

Marion Porath

I have had many wonderful teachers, both formal and informal, including my students. However, there is one teacher who has had a sustained and substantive influence on my practice and who always provokes me to think differently about teaching: Professor Gaalen Erickson. I am, and will continue to be, his student.

Anthony Clarke

To all my teachers who tended my tender garden of mindbodyheartsoul. In particular, I dedicate this book to: my first and eternal teacher, my mother (Hahn, Jee-soo, 1915–2004); my daughters, Lumina and Serenna Romanycia, who taught me things about being an educator that only one's children can; my first Philosophy Professor, Dr. Kim, Yong-jung, in Korea, who set me upon a lifelong path of philosophizing; my first graduate supervisor in Philosophy of Education, the late Dr. LeRoy Daniels, whose generosity and kindness catapulted me into the stratosphere of the academy; and to my partner for all seasons, Avraham Cohen, whose teachings overflow my cup.

Heesoon Bai

My whole life, even the parts full of holes, even the parts I now confess as less than holy, has been a sacred adventure of learning and teaching. I have known many teachers, and all my teachers have helped shape who I am and who I am becoming, and I am grateful for all of them, but especially thankful for Ted Aoki, Rita Irwin, and Barry Cameron, extraordinary scholars and mentors, and Madeleine and Mirabelle Reithmeier, my darling and daring granddaughters who remind me daily how to live in the particular moment that is the heart's beat.

Carl Leggo

I can picture her petite build and the grey streak in the front of her short brown hair, she the age of my mother. Inside grade 11 English, Ms. Woolley introduced me to the novel, to writing, to transcendentalist thinkers. More importantly, she sidetracked my melancholy and adolescent discontent with the world for moments so that I was free to live in my imagination and dream the world otherwise.

Karen Meyer

INVOCATION

Speaking of Teaching is a collection of texts about our lives, or should we say our inner lives, as six colleagues who gather regularly and talk about what inspires us inside out. We are teachers of many years. We are also learners who dwell inside particular personal practices, such as art, Daoism, and poetry. Our conversations and writing stay close to the heart of teaching and learning and their intimate connections to a living inquiry of being and creating in the world. The texts we have called 'innerworkings' are expressions and impressions of our conversations across several years as well as our lifelong inquiries of inner work.

The print on the cover of the book that holds our writing is a metaphor for this body of work. While a woodcut print is a tangible artistic product, each print made from the block is not a copy, but rather an original and unique 'impression.' Its making is an intricate process that involves the artist carving away essential parts of the block that will not receive the ink, requiring a simultaneous awareness of form and non-form while 'seeing' the whole design. The empty space created in the print is the 'ma' or interval, invoking the imagination to linger in possibilities that lie in pauses. We see our innerworkings as experiential pauses and invocations that speak of teaching and non-teaching as spaces of awareness and vision.

TABLE OF CONTENTS

Invitation to the Inner World of Educators	1
Foreword	9
Becoming a Daoist Educator	13
The Artistry of Teaching	35
Attending to the World Differently	51
Education for Enlightenment	63
Poetic Inquiry	83
Living Inquiry	109
Having Spoken of Teaching	125
About the Authors	129

AVRAHAM COHEN

INVITATION TO THE INNER WORLD OF EDUCATORS

As a child of 11, just after going to bed one night, I had a revelatory experience. I was suddenly aware that everything in this unimaginably vast universe was interconnected.. I didn't rationally figure this out, nor had I read about it. I felt with absolute certainty that this was the only sensible understanding of the world. This understanding emerged whole in my young consciousness. I explained all this to my six and a half year old brother, Stephen, who was lying in the bed beside me, and as I later discovered was asleep during my animated explanation. I didn't bother checking to find out if he was awake or not. Since that day long ago, I have searched for wholeness and clarity about everything, including what it is to educate and to be educated. As well, I have been in search of people with whom I can share and further work on my vision of education. It dawned on me after many years, and after immense personal struggles and concerns about what might be wrong with me, that I didn't seem to see the world as most people did, that my vision was often at odds with everyone else's, which certainly helped clarify why it had not been easy to find kindred spirits. As life went along, I have found some kindred spirits here and there, and when I engaged in my doctoral work in the Faculty of Education at the University of British Columbia, I was fortunate to come across like-minded and innovative scholars, including, notably, those who eventually were the members of my thesis supervisory committee, Karen, Carl, and Tony. Marion, who was not on my committee but served as a mentor, and Heesoon, who is of like-mind and my companion in all things.

I have been a psychotherapist for many years, although involved in various forms of delivering education as well. Since 2001, I have been a faculty member at City University of Seattle at the Vancouver BC, Canada site in the Master's of Counselling Program. Previously I taught at a community college in a certificate program in counselling. In my work as a psychotherapist I work with individuals, most of whom would likely have been assessed as gifted as children, and while they most frequently come to work on personal and relational issues, what invariably emerges is how they can access their optimal potential. My intention is to create an environment within which their creative potential and wholeness is invited to emerge. I pay attention to what is there, and perhaps, most importantly, what is not there and which is somehow making itself known by way of small flickers. An outcome of my own sensitivity and inner work (Cohen, 2009) is an enhanced ability to notice these flickers at whatever level of subtlety they appear. My training and experience provides me with methods with which I can facilitate the growth of these flickers into full and embodied realities. Surprisingly, perhaps, some of the richest veins initially show up as the darkest and most objectionable personal material. This material may appear as unwelcome and unacceptable thoughts and feelings, body symptoms, relationship problems, or as 'problems' in the world. As well, I invite people to share their dreams (and nightmares)—both the day and night varieties. Inner work on dreaming processes and content is laden with the potential that lies within individuals, relationships, communities, and world circumstances. Perhaps a small example about dream work will give you an idea of what unlocking a mystery within a dream can look like.

> Many years ago I was working with a young woman who shared a dream. As she described it, she mentioned that there seemed to be something behind her and slightly to the right, and she stated emphatically that she didn't think this was important. I asked if she was open to spending a few minutes checking this 'thing' out. She was a little skeptical but agreed to do so. I had her get up from the chair and go and stand where this thing seemed to be. I had her 'feel' her way into this place and space, and suggested that she speak a few words from that place. What emerged was the loss of her maternal grandmother to whom she had felt incredibly close and whose loss had been devastating to her as a 12-year old girl. She had never grieved this immense loss. Her mother had no ability to help her with this at the time, as she did not know how, and she was, no doubt, overwhelmed with the loss herself. What emerged were her wounds and her potential that was tied up in not feeling this loss. Her inner relationship with her grandmother began to heal and grow, and she was able to enrol her grandmother as an ally and support for her life in both her inner and outer worlds.

I see dreams as unexpressed possibilities in individuals, relationships, communities, classrooms, the world, and specifically in groups such as ours. Our book, and its potential contribution, is one small manifestation of this dream emergence.

Similarly, groups represent unrealized dreams and possibilities. Our group is an excellent example of this. At the outset we had a better starting point than most groups. All the members knew and had positive feelings for each other. Each member of the group knew the others—to greater and lesser degrees. I have worked with groups for many years and have the view that their positive potential is almost invariably untapped. Common mistakes made by groups are: 1) we know each other; 2) we don't need any structure to make the group work; and 3) we deal with stuff when we have to; all great ideas. However, if it worked this simply and easily, then most of us would enjoy being in groups and look forward to them. The reality is that groups are the combined reflections of each person's family background, organizational and institutional experiences, and commonly, people have been participants in group environments and their experience is all too familiar; groups that are frustrating to be in, deadening, unable to perform well, and for some members intimidating and frightening. My intent with the processes that I introduced to the group (Cohen, 2009) was to set up conditions that would predispose the group to be authentic in the moment, get to know each other in a deeper way, develop the community dimension of the group, and create conditions that would allow the group to go well beyond mere prevention and into the farthest reaches of individual and collective creativity, care, and being. I know that our group members agree that these possibilities are being realized. This book is one significant manifestation of this.

For me, the purpose of education is to engage in a process of enlightenment that pervades all aspects of life, emanates from the core of being, and manifests through the personal, the relational, and the professional dimensions. Given the complexity and enormity, not to mention mystery, of reality, our mind-body-heart-spirit, that is, our whole being, needs to be very spacious, open, wide awake, sensitive and responsive, and loving to be able to embrace reality. My vision of education is a quest for becoming whole enough and loving enough to fully embrace reality, which I believe maps well onto becoming enlightened.

As I have come to know each group member in more substantial ways, I have become increasingly convinced that their success as excellent educators is related to their personal work on their own growth and enlightenment: that is, that they are on their own personal quest for becoming whole, heart-full, deeply relational, honest and courageous, loving, compassionate, creative, and life-embracing. My statement here does not just reflect my subjective bias as a former student! In each case, our success as teachers was institutionally validated: Everyone in our group received the top university teaching award from their institution. Anthony (Tony) Clarke, in addition to the university teaching award, received the prestigious National 3M Teaching Fellowship in 2010. All of our group members have received additional recognitions that are too numerous to mention. As well, in case I appear to be only an admiring outsider to this group of pedagogues, allow me to mention on my own behalf, that I too have received recognition as an educator. I have received the British Columbia Association of Clinical Counsellors President's Award for Distinguished Contributions to the Scholarship and Discipline of Counselling, and, most recently, was appointed as Principal Faculty from City University of Seattle, which signifies institutional recognition of my contributions that have exceeded standards over an extended period of time.

My initial contribution to our group was seeing that there was some kind of connection among these educators working on themselves and their practice and receiving university teaching awards. I presented to these professors my insight about this connection as a working hypothesis, and suggested that we form a group to test it. This is how our group dialogue started, and which, six years later, has culminated in the publication of this book.

I had most positive, encouraging, and supportive relationships with my academic supervisors, and I realized that not everyone in graduate school was having this kind of experience. In anticipating my graduation, I wondered if I would have any regular contact at all with my professors after graduation. I felt that losing contact with them would signify a personal loss. Not only that, I was at that point becoming very curious about what it is that these professors had in common that distinguished them as highly esteemed excellent educators. I was beginning to form my aforementioned 'hypothesis.' One day after my PhD oral examination I was walking with Karen Meyer on the University of British Columbia campus. I told her of my interest in investigating what it was that made for exceptional educators: educators who are loved by their students for both their personal and scholarly abilities. I shared with her my view that it was personal qualities that formed the bases for success as an educator, and that I believed that these qualities were an outcome of personal inner work. I told her that I was interested in exploring this idea with a group. I asked if she would have any interest in such a project. To my surprise, she answered without a pause, "Yes." We discussed further and agreed that Carl and Tony should be invited as well, and I added that I thought Marion would also be an important member. She agreed. I went home and told Heesoon about my discussion with Karen. Heesoon rarely volunteers for anything as she always has too much school related work going on at any given time. Again, another very surprising response from her, "I want to be part of your group." That was the beginning of this little group of university educators, and our group has now been meeting regularly for over six years. We have presented our collective work to sometimes standing room only audiences at the 2008 Annual Investigating Our Practices Conference at UBC in the Faculty of Education, the Curriculum and Curriculum Studies division at the 2008 Annual Conference for the Canadian Society for the Study of Education, and the 2009 Annual Conference of the American Educational Research Association. It was apparent that we were speaking to something that was a great fascination for numerous educators.

Our meetings have been stimulating, creative, encouraging, and supportive. We have come to know each other better, and it is my strong impression that we have had the kinds of conversations that professors don't usually have with their colleagues. These conversations have been both personal and scholarly, and most importantly in my view, integrate the personal and the scholarly. The quality of the group was expressed, from the beginning, as a vivifying energy that seems ever-present when we are together. Again, my impression is that our conversations and interaction transcended the more usual and compartmentalized boundaries for professionals, and that this transcendence is essential to the energy's presence. We were integrating what is usually viewed as dissociated and/or adversarial dimensions in the academy, and elsewhere: intellectual versus emotional and the somatic, critical versus creative, and professional versus personal, theoretical versus contemplative.

Throughout our group process, it has become increasingly obvious to me that we as educators are in the very special position of constantly receiving feedback from colleagues, students, and clients with whom we work: feedback that shows us who we are in the moment, each and every moment, what is in us that obscures who we are and our potential, and how we are in contact or not in contact with the world. I say that especially for myself as both educator and psychotherapist. I see that the members of our group teach from a core place within themselves and with a view that prioritizes personal and professional growth as personally and pedagogically integrated and important.

At the beginning of the group's formation, I was somewhat intimidated by and simultaneously very appreciative of the immense accomplishments of our group's members. I was uncertain about my role as leader of a group who for me were clearly my academic superiors both in experience and scholarship. I wondered how I could go from student to leader of this group. Given my uncertainty, I was deeply impressed by their willingness, and even urging, that I take on this role, which I have increasingly been able to grow into. I eventually began to see that I had some offerings of value for the group. It has been my observation that educators are constantly in groups and yet have little or no experience or education that will prepare them to identify and facilitate group process and the associated group dynamics within a classroom. As a psychotherapist and counsellor I brought many years of professional experience in facilitating groups to our group with some obvious positive results.

Karen related hearing the Canadian singer and songwriter, Neil Young, speak about song writing. He said something to the effect of 'you recognize it, you get out of the way, and it comes forth.' I believe the 'it' that is referred to is the emergence of the daemon, the truest expression that can come from a being in the moment. I further believe that a major part of the magic of our group, and of each of us in a classroom, is that in our presence the individual and collective daemons are invited out at a high frequency rate. This experience is perhaps best described in contrast to the oft-heard calls for accountability in the academy. The experience of emergence is unaccountable.

MUSINGS AND REFLECTIONS ON THE GROUP MEMBERS

Many impressions of our group members have emerged prior to and over the life span of the group. I will share a few here. My intent here is to share through my eyes with you, the reader, my knowing of them because I feel knowing an author in a more personal way is very helpful in understanding their work.

Carl—perhaps one of the most scholarly, erudite, and personally encouraging people I have ever met. He has gifted our group with his vast knowledge of language, writing, form, and almost anything else that is worthy of knowing. On a personal level he has shown me a great wisdom that is combined with care for others. From the personal sharing in our group I have found out how greatly moved he is by his two granddaughters. He never fails to share with us some adventure with them that has touched him deeply. When his first granddaughter, Madeleine, was born he told us, "I am in love; in love with Madeleine." I love his exuberance. Contained within his consciousness, along with his great love for his granddaughters, are his consummate abilities as a teacher and scholar. He has supervised and graduated countless numbers of graduate students. He also demonstrates an unfailing goodness of heart and a remarkable resilience in the face of any adversity. He is most unlikely in my experience to say a bad word about anybody even when it seems obvious to me that the situation and the people he had to deal with were not treating him in the fairest or kindest ways. I would be remiss if I did not mention that Carl is a prolific and well-published poet. Poetry flows out of him anywhere anytime. He inhabits the consciousness of the poetics. I can hear his words, complete with a poetic Newfoundland lilt, in my consciousness at this moment, "What the world needs is more poetry!"

Karen—perhaps the fact that Karen has recently returned from Kenya where she worked with teachers in a Somali refugee camp is a most telling demonstration of Karen's nature. She has shown me a rare depth of feeling and compassion for others that permeates her way of being wherever she is and whatever she is doing. She has gone through an extraordinarily tough passage in her role twice as a She She has gone through extraordinarily tough passage in two different department head positions. She shared her personal struggle without ever crossing lines that ought not to be crossed. Her sharing with us gained her emotional support from the group and modelled the potential for disclosure from a vulnerable place that was key to facilitating a deepening of the group's intimacy and growth. I have come to know and admire in a deep way Karen's commitment to not being coerced into conforming to aspects of the academy that do not fit with her personal ethics. She has stuck to her path of Living Inquiry—a paradigm that she has developed—that includes writing within that paradigm and moving increasingly away from the kind of scholarship that for her lacks vitality to a writing form that is existentially meaningful and alive. Her warmth and care for others is impossible to miss. I am prone to quoting a particular statement of Karen's with respect to students, "My job is to see their gifts and help them to emerge." Karen has been gifting the group with her outpouring of creative visions, perceptions, and problem solving, not to mention her artistic sensibilities about everything. Our group's research has been modelled after Karen's Living Inquiry.

Marion—she has an artistic side that had not had an opportunity for a fuller expression. During the time our group has been meeting, there has been a major shift for Marion with respect to her emergence as an artist. It seems that the emphasis in our group on doing what was congruent with each of our own deepest needs and most natural ways of being had an overt influence on Marion. She has over the last two years taken print making courses at Emily Carr University in Vancouver BC. She has uncovered her talents in this area, and today, she is not shy of identifying herself as an artist. The first time she showed us her work we were all quick to recognize her risk, creativity, and talent, and we immediately moved towards including her creative work as part of this book. Her work is on the book's cover and appears throughout. As well, she has taken to heart her own leanings and the consistent message that the group has been conveying about the importance of looking after oneself. She has cut her faculty position to half time in order to have more time for art and what nurtures her soul and that is outside the academic realm. Marion is consistently positive, validating, and energetic in her support of the group and its undertakings. A highly organized person, she has been the person most likely to recall the details of anything we have decided as a group. Of course, I need to mention that Marion is an international figure in the areas of Problem Based Learning and Gifted Children. A supreme academic, Marion has in her distinguished career been a most dedicated and diligent scholar, and is highly respected as a teacher and graduate student supervisor.

Tony—not that there is any stereotyped image of how a distinguished university professor should be these days, but to my possibly biased perception, Tony stands quietly apart from the crowd even while standing in the midst of it and looking very much like a regular member. He has shared with us stories of his not too distinguished past as a student in school in Australia! Tony is a well-published and highly respected scholar. He is regularly invited to present his work internationally. He is particularly well known for his work on reflective practice and on education for field supervisors of pre-service teachers. He is good humoured, full of jokes, easy-going, gentle-mannered, and always humble. I always feel at ease in his presence. He has announced at times, somewhat to the group's surprise and entertainment, his doubts as to whether he has an inner life. He has challenged the group with his honest questions and concerns about what we are doing as scholars, and what he is doing in relation to our projects. The group has been hugely appreciative of these critical challenges and our work has become stronger in response. Tony has been an athlete all his life. He is a former gymnast. I am absolutely impressed by his bike riding stamina, 365 days a year—to school and to most other appointments. I have suggested to him that I will write an article titled, *The Fit Academic*, and that he will be the case example. He is in my view a great example of mind-body integration. My experience has been that he is a very supportive and calming influence in tough and challenging situations, and he will be the one to make an observation that cuts through to core of an issue.

Heesoon—I will be even less objective about Heesoon than the other members of our group, as she is my partner in all things. Heesoon is a consummate scholar in her field of Philosophy of Education, and is highly respected and sought-after as a graduate student supervisor. She is also a scholar and practitioner of Buddhist and Daoist practices. She brings to our group her absolutely amazing beaming and uplifting energy along with incisive and creative comments and ideas. She is currently adding to her repertoire of learning by immersing herself in formal studies at my university in my professional field—counselling. She has brought the insights she is gaining through her studies to the group and to very good effect. The merging of eastern philosophy and humanistic-existential counselling theory and practice has enriched our relationship in very many ways and has brought insight to our group that has enhanced our experience and scholarly work.

And on behalf of myself: I have brought the ideas and practices of inner work to the group. Carl once told me that he feels that the group trusts that I "will keep the group safe and push us" and that "something magical has emerged because I called the group together." My personal interests in inner work have evolved and developed over many decades. Inner work is a practice that involves noticing and attending to inner experience and working with these experiences using any one or more of a variety of approaches, including contemplative practices and psychotherapy. An important awareness for me is that within groups, and certainly this includes classroom groups, there is a multiplicity of inner events going on constantly. Inner world experiences have an impact on each person's ability and ways of participation in the classroom environment. The educator's inner experiences and their outward manifestations have a central influence on the atmosphere and vitality of the classroom experience. I brought to the group my experience and knowledge about these processes, inner life awareness, and inner work. This seems to have been a valued contribution for our group and was a central focus of our work together and our increasingly interconnected beingness.

As you read the essays in this book, you will surely get a feel for the manifestations of our attention to the human dimension within our group and to each of us individually, and how this has manifested in the pedagogical offerings of each of us. It is our hope that our writings will encourage you to deepen your own inner work in relation to your pedagogical practice.

REFERENCES

Cohen, A. (2009). *Gateway to the Dao-field: Essays for the awakening educator*. Amherst, NY: Cambria.

GARY POOLE

FOREWORD

I am in strong agreement with those who suggest that the single best way to improve teaching in post-secondary institutions is to provide opportunities for people to talk to one another about their teaching (e.g., Meyer, 2008). Thoughtful and intelligent people can gain important insights when they share ideas and experiences.

As simple as this may sound, the assertion that allowing for dialogue is the single best method for improving teaching is not without its questions that need answering. As someone who has spent a good deal of his career trying to facilitate this dialogue, these questions have challenged me for some time. Happily, *Speaking of Teaching* has provided me with some answers. It is a book, after all, that grew from conversations—over tea and scones, over meetings to plan presentations, and over years.

One of the questions I appreciated getting some answers to concerns just what should be the topics of our conversations when we talk about teaching. Teaching is a richly multifaceted endeavour. It isn't always easy to know just where we should focus our thinking and our dialogue. In *Speaking of Teaching*, six educators talk about their inner selves. They bring the inside out for their own self-exploration. And they bring the inside out for us to view and learn from. They also question the boundaries between the inner and the outer and whether existence can be dichotomized in this way.

What we talk about, then, is the product of digging down into our values, our sense of self, and our sense of others. An important topic in conversations about teaching is the products of our inner work. This is more challenging than discussions of teaching techniques or impressions of 'students these days.' Discussions of the products of inner work require impressive degrees of honesty and courage. There is little point in discussing simply what we think people want to hear about teaching when we know that the inner work yields more intricate content.

The exploration of inner work via dialogue can render one vulnerable. What if our values need to be seriously questioned? What if our inner selves are the products of decades of socialization that effectively feeds into an unsustainable status quo? The authors of *Speaking of Teaching* assert that such realizations are quite likely when one engages in this inner work, and we need to be ready to face them.

As vulnerable as such work might make us feel, it is absolutely essential work for educators. Avraham Cohen describes the energy he feels when he enters a classroom with a keen awareness of his inner self. He provides an example to remind us that this awareness, and the continual revisiting of the self—while in the moment can be challenging, but nonetheless necessary—as we ask, "Am I responding honestly here? Am I supporting my students in ways that are true to my values as an educator?" These questions help me better understand just what we should be talking about when we talk about teaching.

We tend to think that being in the present is a path to relaxation and stress-free existence. There is some merit to this view, given that much of our stress and worry comes from either pessimistic anticipation of the future or what one of my professors in graduate school called endless post-mortems of the past. In light of these possibilities, the present seems calmer. Yet, there is no reason to assume that the present isn't as tumultuous as what we create or re-create when thinking about our past and future. Heesoon Bai reminds us of this, as does Cohen's in-class example of a student whose behaviour he thought needed to be given attention.

For educators, being in the present demands a willingness to confront the here and now. Again, this confrontation requires courage, as does the reflection that follows it. Why? Perhaps we are never fully adequate in a profession for which there is no ceiling on adequacy. We can always get better, and our inner work exposes the gap between who we are and who we could be. In *Speaking of Teaching*, we are invited to explore the emotions associated with such inner work and the realization that there are always ways that we can get better at what we do. We need to be at peace with this process or it will become too aversive to manage.

This leads to my second question: How should we talk about teaching? Again, *Speaking of Teaching* provides numerous helpful examples. It is possible that the inner work is best expressed artistically, partly because teaching itself is artful, and partly because the connections among words, images, and emotions afforded by artistic expression capture so well those things we find in teaching. It is as though art is a manifestation of the energy that Avraham Cohen feels when he walks into a classroom. It seems perfectly natural to me, therefore, to find so much artistic expression in this book, from the work of Marion Porath and Karen Meyer to the poetry of Carl Leggo.

That said, I must confess that artistic expression has not been commonplace in the countless workshops I have facilitated in higher education. We have explored metaphors and symbols on occasion, but that represents a brief foray into what could be a very rich domain. Perhaps I have assumed that my colleagues did not come to these sessions with the expectation that they would be discussing emotional aspects of their work as teachers. Perhaps they did not expect to do inner work. Clearly, I have inner work to do in this regard.

Whatever participants' expectations were, *Speaking of Teaching* has encouraged me to invite more artistic expression into the ways we talk about teaching. This will be an interesting thing to take on in my home Faculty of Medicine.

When should we talk about teaching? Tony Clarke's chapter reminds me that there is no 'off switch' for the parts of our brain that guide us as educators. In remote Canadian parkland, a chance encounter sheds light on the nature of teaching and learning. Pedagogy, it appears, is as ubiquitous as learning itself. The authors of *Speaking of Teaching* would probably assert that there is no 'off switch' for the inner work of the educator either.

FOREWORD

The inner work, and the habits of mind that support it, define and re-define us as educators. So do our conversations with others who are engaged in the same work. There should be no prescribed time for this work or for the conversations that relate to it. In my current position at our university, I will be bringing colleagues together to talk about our teaching. I would like these conversations to be informal, in that there will be little in the way of expected script. We might pick a topic, like assessment, or self-directed learning, but there will be no presentations on such topics. As keen as I am on these events, I would be very disappointed if my colleagues thought that their conversations about teaching were restricted to such moments. Our building's architecture affords chance meetings, and I hope that we can be opportunistic in our use of such moments to talk about our work as teachers.

And, finally, how shall we act upon our conversations about teaching—of both the intrapersonal and interpersonal variety? Effective inner work stimulates some degree of transformation. *Speaking of Teaching* reminds us that we don't just attempt to understand our inner selves; we question those selves. When we do, we may come to Heesoon Bai's conclusion that there are internalized values that are problematic—contributing to a civilization that is untenable and unsustainable. More courage is required as our inner work becomes a cycle of self-exploration and improvement. This process moves us beyond understanding who we are to considering who we can be.

This honest investigation of who we can be is, for me, the central challenge tacitly presented in *Speaking of Teaching*. It is why the book needs to be read and re-read, and why groups like the one that spawned this book should be commonplace in higher education and beyond.

REFERENCES

Meyer, E. (2008, April). Helping Our Students: Learning, Metalearning, and Threshold Concepts. Symposium on Teaching and Learning Research in Higher Education. The Higher Education Quality Council of Ontario (HEQCO)

INNERWORKINGS

AVRAHAM COHEN

BECOMING A DAOIST EDUCATOR

I have long been fascinated with eastern esoteric ideas and writings that are considered by others enigmatic but I find them quite intelligible and profoundly so . . .

AND, JUST WHAT DID I LEARN IN SCHOOL TODAY?

Learning is the gate to attainment of the Way. Therefore learning is the gate, not the house. When you see the gate, do not think it is the house. You have to go through the gate to get to the house, which is inside, behind it. (Musashi & Munenori, 2005, p. 100)

I have long been fascinated with eastern ideas, writings and practices that others may find enigmatic. Somehow I find them quite intelligible and even profoundly so. In fact, I often have trouble understanding rational philosophical writings from the west that for others are clear and self-evident in their meaning!

Chapter One of Dao De Jing (Ames & Hall, 2003) contains the following:

Together they are called obscure.
The obscurest of the obscure,
They are the swinging gateways of the manifold mysteries. (p. 77)

In another translation of chapter one, (Lao Tzu, 1989) the following:

The Tao that can be told is not the eternal Tao.
The name that can be named is not the eternal name.
The nameless is the beginning of heaven and earth.
Darkness within darkness.
The gate to all mystery. (p. 1)

The Dao is pervasive; it is everywhere. Any efforts to put a finger on the Dao will obscure it. Others may find all this obscure. Somehow I find it all clear!

I have studied Zen and Daoist philosophy (e.g., Cleary, 1978; Lao Tsu, 1989; Clarke, 2000: Magid, 2002/2003), applying them to everyday life, and trying to practice them with every conscious breath (Cohen, 2009). This effort has taken me to various forms of inner and outer work, including Iyengar yoga (Iyengar, 1965), aikido (Ueshiba, 2002), Daoist practices (Chia, 2002), weight training, running, and of course meditation (Hahn, 2001) in various forms. I would also say, with increasing conviction, that my work in psychotherapy as well as my university teaching is an extension of my inner and outer work. My psychotherapy work is an awareness practice in Zen and Dao that allows me to catch glimpses into the deeper fabric of life and see the threads of my own nature and those of others woven into it, sometimes barely visible through tight knots and tangles of broken fibre.

Awa Kenzo, the archery master (as cited in Stevens, 2007), stated the following with which I resonate deeply: "The essence of Buddhism is not meditation or liberation from samsara. It is kensho, 'seeing into your nature'" (p. 44). Another way of understanding the Dao-Field is as a metaphor, which points to how we are all inter-connected and how the well-being of all aspects of the world are connected to all beings and all things. The evidence of this interconnection is not a rational process, nor is it irrational. It sits outside the rational/irrational paradigms (i.e., western philosophy), and is best known experientially by edging up towards reality as it actually is. My essay in this volume, *Becoming a Daoist Educator: The Pedagogy of Wu-Wei*, is both the outcome and direction pointer towards what I believe to be of real value in the education of students, and perhaps more importantly, of ourselves as educators.

I think it important to add that my views about and practice of counselling and psychotherapy, which have been very influential in my work on the human dimension in education and the associated and integral nature of what it is to be human, are located at and beyond the margins of the mainstream of this profession. These views have grown out of my personal history, which was essentially a deep struggle to fit in, to know and be myself, whatever that might mean or look like, my own personal search for meaning, and my desire for substantial connection with other human beings. At some point I clearly recognized that whatever it might take to fit into the mainstream, I did not seem to have it. Over time I recognized increasingly that I could not afford to do anything that conflicted with becoming other than what is authentic to me. I became aware over time that my personal sensitivities and sensibilities mitigated strongly against my pursuing anything other than this path, if I wished to live a fulfilling, meaningful, and reasonably healthy life physically and psychologically. My views and feelings were further confirmed when I fully immersed myself in the Human Potential Movement (Rogers, 1965; Leonard, 1968; Bugental, 1987; Mindell, 1985; Moustakas, 1995) during the 1970s. This movement arose for many reasons, including as a reaction to Freud's work on psychoanalysis that was seen as having too much emphasis on intellectual insight and not enough connection to the feeling dimension and its integration with the intellect. As well, there was a reaction to the emphasis in behaviouristic therapies that seemed to view human beings deterministically and as somewhat mechanistic entities. The Human Potential Movement emphasized the humane, emotions, aliveness, the spiritual dimension, growth potential, relational and embodied dimensions, along with a view that free will was a possibility to be enacted by human beings.

In this short introduction my intent was to provide some clues as to what I have brought into my work in education, the work of our group, and the work within our group.

My own narrative is about my own re/search into comm/union with the Dao: felt/known inter-being with all things. To sum up my inner experience and its relationship to my educational practice:

When I Am One

what else could i be?
am i then part of everything?
am i indeed, everything?
no, that's not possible!
and yet, i do feel that glimmering shimmering that suggests
ever so quietly,
immense possibility. . .

REFERENCES

Ames, R. T., & Hall, D. L. (2003). *Daodejing: Making this life significant* (A philosophical translation). Toronto, ON: Ballantine.

Bugental, J. F. T. (1987). The art of the psychotherapist: How to develop the skills that take psychotherapy beyond science. New York: Norton.

Chia, M. (2002). Bone marrow nei kung: Taoist techniques for rejuvenating the blood and bone. Rochester, Vermont: Destiny Books.

Clarke, J. J. (2000). The Tao of the west: Western transformation of Taoist thought. London: Routledge.

Cleary, T. (Ed.). (1978). *The original face: An anthology of rinzai Zen*. (T. Cleary, Trans.). New York: Grove.

Cohen, A. (2009). Gateway to the Dao-Field: Essays for the awakening educator. Jamestown, NY: Cambria.

Hahn, T. N. (2001). *Thich Nhat Hahn: Essential writings*. Maryknoll, NY: Orbis Books.

Iyengar, B. K. S. (1965). *Light on yoga*. Chicago, Ill: George Allen & Unwin.

Leonard, G. (1968). *Education and ecstasy*. New York: Dell.

Lao Tsu. (1989). *Tao Te Ching* (G. Feng & J. English, Trans.). Toronto, Canada: Random House.

Magid, B. (2002/2003). Ordinary mind: Exploring the common ground of Zen and psychoanalysis. Sommerville, MA: Wisdom.

Mindell, Arnold (1985). *Working with the dreaming body*. San Francisco CA: Harper.

Moustakas, C. (1995). *Being-in, being-for, being-with*. Northvale, NJ: Jason Aronson.

Musashi, M., & Munenori, Y. (2005). *The book of five rings: A classic text on the Japanese way of the sword*. (T. Cleary, Trans.). Boston: Shambhala.

Rogers, C. (1965). *Client-centered therapy*. Houghton Mifflin.

Stevens, J. (2007). Zen bow, Zen arrow: The life and teachings of Awa Kenzo, the archery master from Zen in the art of archery. Boston: Shambhala.

Ueshiba, M. (2002). *The art of peace* (J. Stevens, Ed. & Trans.). Boston MA: Shambhala.

BECOMING A DAOIST EDUCATOR:
THE PEDAGOGY OF WU-WEI

Inner Life within the Dao-Field

There is no other task but to know your own original face. This is called independence; the spirit is clear and free. If you say there is some particular doctrine or patriarchy, you'll be totally cheated. Just look into your heart; there is no transcendental clarity. Just have no greed and no dependency and you will immediately attain certainty. (Yen-t'ou, 828–887, as cited in Cleary, 1998, p. 32)

When I walk into a classroom I almost invariably feel that I am in just the right place. I love being in classrooms as an educator. I feel that it is my place. I am aware that I also bring a Shadow along with me and that this Shadow has reluctance about being there, but for now I will speak about the light and just remember that the Shadow is never far away, even now. Even though this Shadow aspect comes along, it is mixed in with my love of being there and knowing that my students and I are there to do something together, but even more importantly I am excited about the fact that we will be there together. I have a sense of being in a field of energy, a Dao-Field, a field that at once holds us and that we simultaneously constitute. For me the class starts even before I enter the room. I am already working with my own energy and the energy of the group prior to arriving in the room. I am thinking, not so much about curriculum matters, but about the individuals and the group as a whole. I am remembering processes and events. I am imagining possibilities. Dialogues are already occurring in my inner world. I am seeing students and feeling their presence. I feel whole and energized. I can't wait to get there. When I walk in I notice who is there, get a feel for their space, and begin conveying my space to them and engage in a process of connecting. I am tuned to the nuance and detail of the process with individuals and with the group as a whole. I watch as the group gathers. I see who is talking to whom. I am checking the energy, or at least my perception of the energy, of each person and of the group as a whole. By the time the class begins I already have established a connection with each person either directly or within myself. I am also tuned into myself. I can feel my heart beat. My breathing is conscious. I am noticing small flickers of feeling and body language. I am looking for what is invisible; what is not there. For example, is a person who is normally smiling and gregarious quiet? I am observing what is actually in the room and I am making meaning of what I perceive. I am aware of the meanings that emerge for me and I hold these loosely. I am prepared to find out that what I see and how I understand it is not the way it is. My original face, my nature, shows up in the matrix of the classroom.

I believe that this experience is not very common amongst educators. More frequently I believe it is the case that teachers at all levels come into classrooms fearful, stressed, and uncertain; uncertain in a way that is not helpful to them or their students. In this chapter, I will in various ways be acknowledging the uncertainty that is a central spirit in Daoist and Zen practice, practices that cultivate an uncertainty, a not-knowing, that is full of possibility and qi, or life energy. The state of openness that exemplifies wu-wei, a state of non-doing, of emptiness, not to be confused with dullness, rather it describes a state of alertness, a readiness for anything including the full use of knowledge and experience that the educator has available in-the-moment within him or herself, and an awakened capacity to respond in the moment to what students bring into the classroom, individually and collectively. It is a way of heart-fullness that engages readily and actively with the human dimension in a deep and caring way.

Here is an example of observation, personal experience, and personal meaning-making based on a voice from the classroom of the world:

> *I am out for a run. I am passing a white-haired woman standing on the sidewalk who appears quite elderly. She is supporting herself with a cane. She says something. I can't quite make it out. All at once, her words assemble as a whole in my consciousness. "I wish I could do that."*

There are many possible ways to take this message from a wounded and suffering elder. Perhaps she is just making idle chit-chat. Maybe she is jealous or even bitter. How I hear her is as a voice from the world. There are many possibilities about her that only she could tell me, but in my inner world she has set off a reminder that I am indeed fortunate. I can run; something that I could take for granted. For the moment I do not. I am not so young as I used to be, yet I am able to run easily, painlessly, for an extended period of time. I can enjoy the pleasure of my body's ability to move through the world in this energetic way. I feel also my good fortune to understand this chance encounter as I do. I have come to this way of understanding through a long process of inner work; a process of ongoing inner reflection on my life experience, how life has shaped and mis-shaped me, and how I have worked on my inner experiences through various reflective processes to recover my self, my sensitivities, my ability to see, feel, taste, touch, and relate to the world. The world is alive in the moment. This is the pedagogy of the street, of the world, and of the elder. I have recovered my ability to perceive through my senses and their inter-being with my consciousness. This is one small example of my beingness in the world and it is also the consciousness that I bring to classroom, at least, in my best moments. Classrooms are full of these moments. The only question is whether you or I are in a condition to notice and respond to them as they unfold.

My writing in this chapter is as much as possible in the spirit of my approach to classroom practice. I will speak to you, the reader, as directly as possible, and with my sense of what matters. Now there is a difference. In a classroom I am simultaneously speaking and 'listening' to you and everyone else that is there. By this I mean what I have called multi-dimensional communication construction in the moment (Cohen, 2004), which means that when I am speaking I am aware of feedback and similarly while you are speaking I am 'expressing' myself to you non-verbally. What is different here is that this writing could be viewed as an extended lecture, which is something that I would be unlikely to do in a classroom. I want students to have every opportunity to participate in the conversation; to contribute their knowledge and expertise, to ask questions, and to connect meaningfully with each other and with me. I am hopeful that even though we are experiencing these words in asynchronous time, we are still in a dialogue. I know that I am 'thinkingfeeling' you as I write. I have also chosen to write out of the same energy stream from within which I participate in a classroom, which means that the overall impression may be available even while linearity is not.

WE ARE ALL THE PROBLEM

As Palmer (1998) put it, "We teach who we are" (p. 1). If a teacher is whole, then he or she will teach that, and alternatively, if an educator is not whole, then that will be the lesson. The problem is not that a teacher is less than whole. That is the case for most of us. The problem is being unconscious about the holes in our wholeness and perpetrating the effects of these deficits on others.

I believe that anomie and alienation are pervasive conditions in schools and on university and college campuses and I believe that a central task for education is the transformation of this experience. The signals of trouble are everywhere and continually indicating that anomic and alienated individuals suffer, and in extreme cases will evoke massive suffering for others. I believe that these individuals are separated from their own true nature, from other humans, and from the natural environment. These dark experiences point towards what is possible—the revivifying of these connections as a felt and lived experience. Educators are well situated and have a crucial role, opportunity, and responsibility to attend to the human dimension in educational environments in the service of facilitating the healing and optimal growth of these ruptured connections.

A subtle process of harm can occur insidiously in educational settings, which leads to a destruction of the hearts, minds, and souls of students and educators in our frequently production-oriented and inhumane academic environments. You will see the results of the damage, but not the site, at least not until you look energetically, deeply, and persistently inward. For until you can see clearly enough, you will not see the nature of the suffering of others or that which transpires between yourself and others, and yourself and the environment.

Three major 'locations' where the anomic experience is either engendered or transformed are families, communities, and schools. My focus is on educators and their tremendous opportunity to create and educate for connection in a substantial and meaningful way to self, other, and community.

I believe that in the vast majority of cases, parents and teachers do their best. This does not change the fact that the wounding that occurs is related to their shortcomings. To survive, from an early age, children begin to develop ways of being that lead inexorably to psychic numbing, and those ways become armour-like, serving three different and equally damaging purposes. First, this process of numbing seals, at least to some extent, children's true, vibrant, and sensitive nature inside a shell, second that shell becomes hard, bruising, and damaging to others, and third others are kept at an emotional distance. I-thou (Buber, 1970) relationship does not occur. Privilege is another form of wounding that can create obliviousness to the difficulties of others and in turn a desensitization of feelings to avoid the pain of awareness about the damage privilege can perpetuate for both those with and those without privilege.

My own history in school, from the earliest days, was one of holographic recurrence and enhancement of wounding. I was not encouraged to thrive in elementary or high school and my undergraduate years were mostly torturous. As I matured and became a graduate student, I became skilled at selecting the right teachers and my experience became extremely positive. I witnessed many of my fellow students who were not so skilled in this way suffering greatly. As a young person, I was constantly being re-wounded and did not recognize my experience as wounding. In my work as an educator I have come to see that while the details of my experience differs from others, the patterns and process were and are almost everyone's. I have come to see that school has every bit as much, if not more, capacity to wound and re-wound as do families, religious institutions, and culture, and almost always with the best of intentions.

TEACHERS, GREAT AND ALL

I held the view for a long time that great teachers are inner work practitioners, that is, individuals who are aware of the inner processes and know the landscape of their personal consciousness. Central to this personal consciousness is interest in and emerging awareness of present and historical experiences along with the patterns that these represent and that may be unconsciously and powerfully influential in how he or she is acting in the world. Most certainly, great teachers have a passion and love for their life as educators and there is something that they are aware of. However, it has become apparent that the kind of inner and psychological work that I felt was central in fact is not that prevalent. I have found that teachers who are reflective are more likely to be reflective about their practice as described by Schön (1983/1995). This type of reflective practice is literally a critical look back and review of how a particular experience went in the classroom, the purpose being to evaluate the effectiveness of the practice and to make any changes that seem indicated for future pedagogical practice. While this practice definitely has value, it is not the same as reflection on the inner world of the educator that shines light on the identity of the educator that is implementing the practice. Some teachers just seem to have the right endowments and don't seem to have to work at teaching. Even these 'naturals,' I believe, are doing something that has some relationship to inner work. I have found that they are open to feedback, tend to notice it even in its non-verbal forms, and have a genuine interest in incorporating this feedback into their pedagogy. I believe that inner work (Cohen, 2009) would enhance the practice of even these already gifted educators. Surely, the accomplishments of great athletes, artists, poets, and so on are related to the reality that they are practicing and fine-tuning their already substantial gifts. I believe that a central feature of great teacher's abilities is that they indeed do 'teach who they are.' My contention is that the deeper and broader their awareness of 'who they are' is, the more finely tuned will be their instrument—themselves—and the more nuanced and remarkable will be their pedagogy related to both the relational and curricular aspects of education. I believe that inquiry into what has happened in their lives that has led them to be teachers and to teach in the ways that they do, which are already successful, would lead to an even more refined pedagogy.

> *Ku-Shan was asked, "What is the basic object of investigation?"*
> *He replied, "How one has gotten to such a state." (Cleary, 1998, p. 43)*

In my classroom I intend to demonstrate the effects of inner work. In conjunction with inner work I want to create an experience within the classroom that is an alternative to what is all too common for students in their lives of being rushed, stressed, distressed, and uneasy. I want to provide them with an ongoing and consistent lived experience of what is possible that is different and more alive and enlivening within themselves, in relationship, and in community. I also want to demonstrate the integration of curriculum material and beingness that brings to life this material by showing and living how it is relevant to their lives—not only outside of class but in the moment in class as well. The latter turns out to be an ongoing pedagogy of being more fully present. My students tell me that they leave the class most often refreshed and rejuvenated, even after a long day of classes preceding our class together.

I have come to see that much of what I do fits well with eastern philosophies and practices. In particular, I find that Daoism and Zen provide beliefs, values, and practices that readily map onto my pedagogical practice. Two central practices in my life are mindfulness meditation and inner work. The former for me is most closely aligned with Zen teachings that are focused on awareness in the moment and the practice of various meditation forms that have helped me develop my abilities in this domain. Inner work I equate more with psychotherapy, which in some sense I believe is a misnomer. I characterize inner work as education about the inner world, the relational world, and the environment within the psychological realm. This form of work that I practice comes under the heading of existential-humanistic practice, which is an approach that builds on strength, seeks the meaning in adversity, and is non-pathologizing. This approach is often done with the help of a therapist and can be done on one's own with practice. The particular focus I have is process-oriented work (Mindell, Amy, 1995; Mindell, Arnold, 1990; 2000). These practices that I have engaged in over many years have given me an insight into my own conditioning and have helped free me, which in turn enables me to be present for what is within the context of my work as an educator. This presence that I bring seems to have an enlivening effect on students who seem predisposed to commit themselves in profound ways to their interests in their own experience and to the subject matter under study. I believe that central to all good practice and living fully is ongoing development of the capacity to be aware, which is about development of consciousness itself, what Arnold Mindell (1988/2009) calls the meta-communicator and some traditions call the observer. I will now describe the underlying philosophy, some inner work process and experience, and the translation into practice.

WHAT IS DAOISM? WHAT IS ZEN? WHAT IS INNER WORK?

GOING BEYOND

When you get to the point where even a thousand people, even ten thousand people, cannot trap you or cage you, this is still not expertise. You must go on to the beyond and activate the transcendental key, never injuring your hand against the sharp edge, bringing everyone in the world to life. (Ying-an, as cited in Cleary, 1998, p. 98)

The sound of one hand clapping
Is not so awesome as it used to be.
I now listen for the sound of
Ten thousand hands clapping as One. (Lao-Tzu's Protégé, as cited in Cohen, 2009)

Being an educator is a direct path opportunity to enlightenment. Every moment in a classroom shines a light on your soul. Daoist, Zen, and inner work practices are all 'methods' of achieving a state of enlightenment. Educators are paid to be in a circumstance that can show us everything we need to know about what is within that is in the way of feeling free (enlightened). I propose that it is not essential to be enlightened, only that being in the process, taking everything that comes my way, as Buber said, "as a question to myself" (as cited by Längle, 2005, public talk, University of British Columbia, Vancouver, BC, Canada), is an important step towards being a great educator and towards enlightenment.

DAOISM

You need companions to travel
To the Isle of Immortals—
It is hard to climb
The azure cliffs alone.
If you take dead stillness for refinement,
The weak water brimming
Will lack a convenient boat. (Sun Bu-er, 119–1182 CE, as cited in Cleary, 1989, p. 87)

Daoism is the term that is closely associated with the writings of the Daoist sage Lao Tzu. The famous text attributed to the sage is the Dao-De-Ching (Tao-te-ching). The origins of this small text are steeped in an intriguing story (Kohn, 1998). Central to certain Daoist practices is the pursuit of great health and longevity. Lao Tzu as a master was presumed to be able to live eternally. When the Qin ruler asked to meet with him so he could be advised about immortality, he was told that Lao Tzu had left because he saw that the Zhou dynasty was declining. Further, when Lao Tzu reached the western frontier he was asked by the guardian of the gate to write down his ideas for him. Lao Tzu obliged, produced a short work, the Dao-De-Ching, and disappeared. Kohn describes further that Lao Tzu he actually made his way to India where his teachings earned him the name Buddha; his teachings became known as Buddhism. This mystery is further enhanced by scholars (e.g., Kohn, 1998; Roth, 1999; Grigg, 1994) who tell us that there never was such a person as Lao Tzu, and that the writings attributed to him are the collective work of many who were in fact the early Daoists.

Notwithstanding the mystery surrounding its origins, Daoism tells us that a sage is one who is in tune with nature, his or her own nature, the environment, and the ineffable Dao. The first chapter of the Dao-de-ching tells us, "The Way that can be told of is not an Unvarying Way" (Waley, 1958, p. 141). There are many variations on the translation of this line, which seems to sum up the entire text and states more or less that whatever you can say about it is not what it is. In my view this suggests that to know that which is, a person must drop all conceptions, preconceptions, and discursivity, and be fully present in an open and alert manner, relaxed, and ready for life.

Daoist pedagogy provides a view of the overall flow and nature of the classroom. This flow is within each individual, within the class as a whole, and is connected to the overall flow of the world and the ineffable. The teacher is the leader and his or her capacity to be aware of and connect with this flow will have a crucial effect of the creation of the classroom atmosphere and experience.

ZEN

Zen is a school of Buddhism that emphasizes the practice of meditation as the key to awakening one's true nature and uncovering one's innate isdom and compassion. (Batchelor, 2001, pp. 0-1)

Zen comes from a Sanskrit word Dhyana, which means meditative state (Batchelor, 2001). Meditation was the main method for the achievement of this state taught by Shakyamuni Buddha. Buddha, the awakened one, lived about 2,500 years ago and taught a process of cultivating the mind that would allow a person to realize their Buddha or enlightened nature. He said that the nature of existence is suffering. Zen teaching is about developing awareness of the illusory and transient nature of life, including both suffering and joy, which are part of human nature. Zen teaches for the emergence of the ability to see and accept what is, and to not be caught up in our ideas of how things are—to see through the illusion of our conceptions. The epitome of Zen practice according to Magid (2002/2005), who is a Zen teacher and a psychoanalyst, is that it has 'nothing' to offer. What he is saying is that Zen practice guarantees nothing, at least in so far as the external world is concerned, unless you consider learning that events in the world are largely beyond your control. What is 'offered' is a way of developing awareness of your inner life and discovering through experience the potentials of this awakening. Magid states:

> As Zen practice continues . . . ceaseless (and futile) efforts to 'fix' oneself and others fade as it becomes obvious that fixing is simply not the answer to human difficulties. When this happens, a person begins to comprehend the crucial difference between "fixing and transforming." (p. x)

Zen is about being with what is, what actually is, not a confused stew of perception and phenomena. It has little to do with doing and everything to do with being, and becoming a being who is awake. Zen pedagogy provides the educator with a way of accessing that aspect of her or his inner world that is non-divided, that is connected with all things. Zen or Zen-like practice provides the educator with the capacity to facilitate inter-being (Hahn, 2001) in the classroom. This interbeing includes the human, the curricular, and the ineffable.

INNER WORK

Inner work is the practice of noticing in the moment the theatre of my own consciousness and working with this inner process in ways that offer transformational possibilities both in the moment and over time.

Inner work needs to be distinguished from inner life. The latter is the awareness, process, and content of the inner world. Inner work is the work that is done on and with these dimensions of the inner world. Inner work refers to all processes that occur within consciousness and the practice of becoming involved with them in a deep way that leads to transformation of your sense of self and felt sense of increased spaciousness. It is evident to me that having the goal of achieving anything in particular is detrimental to the emergence of what is within you—natural and wanting to emerge. The methods of inner work are on a continuum with all practices that have a focus that contrasts with orientations of consciousness that are focused in the outer world. In fact, inner work may not be the best name for these practices as they are really interactive with the continuum of all phenomena. Specifically, inner work is spiritual work and includes meditation processes, various religious practices, and psychological work that is process-oriented and falls under the rubric of the humanistic-existential therapies that are defined by a lack of pathologizing and objectifying of human beings and that looks for the person, the personal, the relational, and the spiritual dimensions within the context of accompaniment and being.

Here is a brief outline of the process of inner work:

- An event in my world ignites an inner experience.
- I notice the inner experience. (This may sound simple, but much of our outer-directed culture mitigates against it.)
- I review the events.
- I reflect on my actions and the actions of other(s) or the events in the world that are non-human related.
- I attempt to break free of continually going over the catalyzing event in order to see the pattern and be open to the feelings, memories, sensations, images, and associations that are associated with the event.
- I allow and invite these associations into awareness.
- I re-experience these associations.
- I begin to identify the conditioned responses that I have.
- I start to identify the conditioned patterns that are the meta-structures of the current time experience that set the process in motion and that are the very same ones that underlie the emerging associations.
- I use my conscious awareness to 'search' for the choices that are becoming available.
- I open to the energy that has been locked up for so long in these conditioned responses.
- I begin to experiment with the choices and freedom that has not become available.
- I work with accepting the vulnerability that comes with being in a new place within myself.

It goes without saying that the process is not usually so linear and tidy as I have laid out here. This outline is to give an idea of the components of the process. As well, inner work processes can take place over very extended time frames, particularly when it comes to work with deeply entrenched archival material.

FIRST REIFICATION, THEN DISINTEGRATION, THEN NEW GROUND

Each separate being in the universe
returns to the common source.
Returning to the source is serenity. (Lao-Tzu, as cited in Mitchell, 1989/1993, p. 15)

An example of inner work related to pedagogical practice based in classroom experience, albeit fictionalized to preserve confidentiality (I might add, based on an experience about which I am not particularly proud), follows:

> I am teaching a class, which overall has gone very well. There is one student who troubles me. On several occasions she has said things that are on the border and perhaps a little beyond what, in my view, fits in with the classroom environment in a post-secondary institution. She is extremely bright as evidenced by her written work and some of her comments in class, and has told me enough of her

background to make it evident that she had an unwholesome and discouraging start to life. For her to even be here seems to be quite an accomplishment.

One day the class is involved in an animated and intense discussion. I look over to the left side of the circle and see this young woman sitting slumped down in her chair with her head on her lap. I attempt to engage with her and inquire if there is a problem. She looks up and replies, "I'm fine" and smiles. The smile does not look right to me, at all. I feel a chill in my body and then I feel a strong surge of energy arising in me. I'm becoming angry. I try again. "You don't seem okay." Again she says, "Nope, I'm fine." The class discussion has come to a halt. All eyes are riveted on this student and me. I say, "I don't think you're okay and your behaviour here is definitely not okay." The atmosphere is now of a consistency that lends itself to visions of a knife attempting to cut it. Some part of my consciousness recognizes that whatever is going on with her and whatever her state, the primary issue is now my state of being and the conditions in this classroom. I feel a pain in my chest. It is mixed with fear. The discussion that we were having had been about an experiential exercise and how it was to be conducted. I mumbled that perhaps we can have a try at the exercise and that perhaps what had just happened might be included in the exercise. Ironically the exercise is about group leadership.

Usually I walk around, listen in, and offer support during these practice opportunities, but today I stay in my chair, vaguely watching for any problems and mostly focused on my inner world. I feel my heart beating. I am aware of my breath. My anger has changed into fear. I almost instantly develop my list of worries: 1) I've ruined the class, which up to now has been going well, 2) I have screwed up 'like I always do,' 3) my poor behaviour will be reported to the program coordinator and I will be dismissed, 4) my reputation will be ruined, and 5) I will never teach anywhere again. I am looking into the jaws of some kind of death and inexorably falling in. I begin to follow my own process. The part of me that observes and is not part of the experience directly is awakening. I recognize my own pattern of catastrophizing and recall that things rarely go the way I have imagined, and almost never are they as bad as I am initially inclined to believe. It occurs to me that this is a sophisticated group. I am certainly not the only one who has noticed that at times something is off about this student. My relationship with this group of students has been positive. They like me. I am aware that I am starting to withdraw my projections.

I breathe and I feel my body pulsing. I am entering early stages of shamatha. A memory occurs. I am in a class. I am 11 years old. The teacher has just caught me trading baseball cards with my friend and confiscated my cards. I am in a fear state. I am frightened at being caught, fearful of punishment, and also that my very precious collection is no longer in my hands. I recall that this teacher refused to give the cards back and I lost them forever. I knew suddenly in the moment what it was like to be on both ends of the power and control, fear and anger, of the teacher. My own fear had dominated the situation. I felt a feeling of compassion for myself, for this young student, and the rest of the students. I felt my body and the energy of my life-force returning. She had received, undeservedly, some of the anger that I had not been able to deliver to that teacher so many years ago. My inner work helped move me outside the binary paradigms of fear and anger, power/control and helplessness.

The exercise is over. I call the students back together. As it turned out, they had not done the exercise at all. The time in small groups has been dominated by the events of the preceding moments in the class. I speak about what has happened in terms that acknowledge the events. I do not interpret or evaluate. I put the experience into the context of the actual and personal experience along with some references that point to the related curriculum material. I acknowledge my vulnerability to the class. They express their concerns, appreciations, and criticisms to me, and to the recipient of my wrath, who showed little response. I suspect she just had too many experiences in her life that required her to distance herself from her emotions and others. Students share their feelings. Most dominant is their appreciation that things have been faced head on and not swept under the carpet or avoided.

This situation was messy. My inner work continued after the class and, in fact, for several months. I was able to validate this student in terms of my written feedback on her very good project that she submitted for the class. I had been able to express an apology to her in the class. I am now less prone to such reactivity in classroom circumstances. I have learned through psychological insight and through the practice of meditation that being with what is, is what matters. What is, the actual moment to moment phenomena, I have come to realize is life unfolding and attempts to change this come from reactivity and are major interferences into what is natural and the flow of life.

This example of classroom experience and inner work is not easy for me to share, but in a very real way, it is an enormous benefit to an educator to make good use of circumstances for her or his own development as a human being. Of course, some may criticize me for my less than exemplary treatment of this student. I have no good response to that. I can say that inadvertently she has contributed to my growth and to the well-being of future students who may not have to experience wrath that does not belong to them. I have only my impressions as to the effect on her. She never spoke about it to me. She was, however, appreciative of the detailed feedback I gave on her project and of the genuine encouragement that was part of that feedback.

This example demonstrates the value of inner work in the spiritual realm that moves along the psychological-spiritual continuum. The classroom as a Dao-Field was sequentially, in place, lost, and regained. My ability to reflect quickly on my experience and regain access was applied. Zen practice of being aware was applied. The container, in Buddhist terms, the Sangha, the community had been set up sufficiently well that it could contain this intense and difficult experience. In fact, the class was even more open and animated subsequently. The student seemed to be more subdued for the duration of the course, which for her may have been the best thing, and in some unspoken way she seemed to be more accepted within the classroom community after this event. The class had gone through an experience together of sitting in the fire and finding out that there are possibilities after difficult experiences and that transiting such an experience collectively was an empowering and enlightening experience. They had the experience of seeing a teacher 'lose it' and own up to that 'failing.' They were able to live the transformational potential of the rupture experience.

Inner work recognizes the continuum of spiritual work that includes the ineffable, the psychological, and the inter-subjective. The view of the egoic and psychological self as either a vehicle for expression of the natural self, the meta-dimensions (Cohen, 2007), or alternatively as a grid that lies over the natural expressions of self and is a suppressant, is recognized and worked with using a range of reflective and humanistic-existential practices.

SUMMING UP NOW

What creates things is formless and stays at the still point of the changeless. Now, whoever gets hold of this and dwells in it alone may not be detained, may not be stopped by things. People like this can inhabit a place where there is not excess, can hide in a space that has no hint of a boundary, and can ramble free and easy from the endings to the beginnings of the ten thousand things. They will be at one with the heart they were born with.
(from The Essential Chuang Tzu, 1998, p. 102)

The human dimension and the very personal aspects of the inner life that deeply affect educators and students are not usually addressed as a primary experience in education and are not a part of the curriculum for teacher education. Those who fall outside the norms are offered tutoring, diagnoses, and treatment with an associated sense of isolation. They are not seen and addressed for being the wounded and suffering humans that they are (Cohen & Bai, 2008). They are not offered an I-Thou possibility as described by Buber (1970), nor are they offered the inclusivity of Deep Democracy (Mindell, Arnold, 2002). No, they are further wounded by being identified as 'not-right.' I believe the help and form in which it is offered serve to further dis-empower many of those who are subject to it.

Educators and education may be as powerful as parents and families in their ability to influence consciousness and values. What I am recommending is that we provide human and humane environments in classrooms and let students decide based on their experience how they wish to live and what matters to them. I propose that the initiator of such environments is the teacher, the educational leader, who if not a sage, is alive to the possibilities of living within the process of becoming so.

If educators do not address these human issues in themselves and in students, existing problems in education will be sustained, and worse, we will fail to take advantage of the great opportunity that exists for shifting the paradigm of how humans live together that is presented daily in classrooms. Not unimportantly, my experience in classrooms that address the human dimension is that curriculum learning proceeds smoothly and comprehensively. Ignoring the inner world and the interconnected field phenomena is a guarantee of the continuance of the wounded and wounding experience. I believe that striving towards an enlightened way of being needs to be at the core of education and development, both personally and professionally for teachers. I will leave you with some thoughts, a vignette of experience, and a dream: As the opening chapter of the Tao Te Ching (Lao-tzu, 1988) suggests, relative to what I have shared with you so far: 'Whatever you can say about it is not what it is.'

And in Chapter 17:

> *That when his task is accomplished, his work done,*
> *Throughout the country everyone says, 'It happened of its own accord.'*
> (Waley, 1958, p. 164)

IN THE WORLD

I am out for a run and as I run by the water at Kitsilano Beach I come across an older Chinese man. He is dressed in black. He has short white hair with a small bald spot in the middle. He is performing a Tai-Chi sequence. His movements are slow and fluid. He is a master. A sense of stillness comes over me. The movements are somehow in concert with my running exertion and the moment is timeless. The sun shines. Birds fly overhead. The world is alive and inter-connected. I know my place.

A DREAM FROM MY INNER AND UNCONSCIOUS WORLD

A group of young boys about 12 years old are meeting with the coach of their football team. He is assuming a 'tough' stance, telling them the expectations for players and the consequences of not meeting those expectations, failures that could lead to dismissal from the team, and so on. The team is going to practice kick-off returns. The boys are split into two groups; one group is to be part of the kick off team and one group part of the receiving team. The ball is kicked and the receiving team bobbles it. The whole sequence starts over again. The kick-off is done again. A grandmotherly figure is suddenly part of the receiving team. She is tall, rangy, and has whitish hair. The ball goes directly to her. She catches it easily and runs directly up the field in a straight line towards the goal line. I keep anticipating that she will pass the ball to one of the boys. She does not. She runs straight up the field, through the whole kick-off team and into the end zone. The coach is nowhere to be seen.

Apparently, the disciplinarian is irrelevant. The young boys cannot handle the job. They have the wisdom to not resist the chi[1] that the grandmother has as she moves through them into the end zone. She has done what would seem to be impossible. A grandmother has run easily and directly through a group of young boys whose task is supposedly to stop her. She has addressed the Gateless Barrier, that which seems impossible, with warrior-like directness and ease. Education

---

[1] This is the vital energy that infuses all things and that is the focus of cultivation within Daoist practices.

presents myriad opportunities to address this Gateless Barrier. Wu-men's Comment:

> For the practice of Zen it is imperative that you pass through the barrier set up by the Ancient Teachers. For subtle realization it is of utmost importance that you cut off the mind road. If you do not pass this barrier of the ancestors, if you do not cut off the mind road, then you are a ghost clinging to bushes and grasses. (Magid, 2002/2005, p. 32)

Classrooms, students, and educators are full of Gateless Barriers. Educators can learn to recognize these barriers, address them, see that in fact they are doorways of great potential, learn to live an increasingly barrierless life, and demonstrate to their students the infinite possibilities of living life as an adventure filled with awe, vitality, fluidity, relationship, and wonder.

REFERENCES

Batchelor, M. (2001). *Zen*. London: Thorsons.
Buber, M. (1970). *I and thou*. New York: Charles Scribner and Sons.
Cleary, T. (Ed.). (1989). *Immortal sisters: Secrets of Taoist women* (T. Cleary, Trans.). Boston: Shambhala.
Cleary, T. (Ed. & Trans.). (1998). *Teachings of Zen*. Boston: Shambhala.
Cohen, A. (2004). Multi-Dimensional Communication Construction in the Moment. *Insights: News for Clinical Counsellors, 15*(3), 12–13, 31–32.
Cohen, A. (2009). Gateway to the Dao-Field: Essays for the Awakening Educator. Youngstown, NY: Cambria.
Cohen, A., & Bai, H. (2008). Suffering loves and needs company: Buddhist and Daoist perspectives on the counsellor as companion. *Canadian Journal of Counselling, 42*(1), 45–56.
Cohen, A., & Porath M. (2007, April). Exceptional Educators: Understanding the Dimensions of their Practice. Paper presented at the AERA 2007 Annual Meeting/Self-Study SIG, Chicago.
Grigg, R. (1994). *The Tao of Zen*. Edison, NJ: Charles E. Tuttle.
Hahn, T. N. (2001). *Thich Nhat Hahn: Essential writings*. Maryknoll, NY: Orbis Books.
Hamill, S. & Seaton, J. P. (Trans.) (1998). *The essential Chuang Tzu* Boston: Shambhala.
Kohn, L. (1998). *The Lao-tzu myth*. In L. Kohn & M. LaFargue (Eds.), Lao-tzu (pp. 41–62). Albany: State University of New York.
Längle, A. (2005, February). ECPS Colloquium, University of British Columbia, Vancouver, BC.
Lao-tzu. (1988). Tao te ching (S. Mitchell, Trans.). New York: Harper & Row.
Lao-tzu. (2008). *Tao-te-ching* (J. Star, Trans.). Toronto, ON: Jeremy P. Tarcher/Penguin. (Original work published 2001)
Magid, B. (2005). *Ordinary mind: Exploring the common ground of Zen and psychoanalysis*. Sommerville, MA: Wisdom. (Original work published 2002)
Mindell, Arnold. (1990). Working on yourself alone: Inner dream body work. New York: Arkana.
Mindell, Amy. (1995). *Metaskills: The spiritual art of therapy*. Tempe, AZ: New Falcon.
Mindell, Arnold. (1988/2009). City shadows: Psychological Interventions in psychiatry. New York: Lao Tse.
Mindell, Arnold. (2000). Quantum mind: The edge between physics and psychology. Oakland, CA: Lao Tse.
Mindell, Arnold. (2002). The deep democracy of open forums: Practical steps to conflict prevention and resolution for the family, workplace, and world. Charlottesville, VA: Hampton Roads.
Mitchell, S. (Ed.). (1993). *The enlightened heart: An anthology of sacred poetry*. New York: HarperPerennial. (Original work published 1989)

Palmer, P. (1998). The courage to teach: Exploring the inner landscape of a teacher's life. New York: Jossey-Bass.
Roth, H. D. (1999). Original Tao: Inward training (nei-yeh) and the foundations of Taoist mysticism. New York: Columbia University
Schön, D. (1995). *The reflective practitioner: How professionals think in action.* New York: BasicBooks. (Original work published 1983)
Waley, A. (1958). The Way and its power: A study of the Tao Te Ching and its place in Chinese Thought (A. Waley, Trans.). New York: Evergreen.

INNERWORKINGS

MARION PORATH

THE ARTISTRY OF TEACHING

After a long career in education and several periods of reflection on what makes good teaching I was at a point where, in hindsight, those reflections were kaleidoscopic . . .

THE ARTISTRY OF TEACHING

After a long career in education and several periods of reflection on what makes good teaching I was at a point where, in hindsight, those reflections were kaleidoscopic. Tiny, beautiful fragments of shape and colour, emerging patterns, ideas tumbling about in a tube, constantly changing. I seemed to be searching—artistically—for a coherent image. Hints appeared in my academic work. I wrote about teaching as a virtuoso performance, bringing my background in cognitive developmental psychology to bear to articulate the process, form, and nature of this virtuosity. Artistry crept in, colouring my more usual cognitive vocabulary. Using words and phrases like 'interpretive,' 'orchestration,' 'artisans,' 'aesthetics of educational environments,' and 'rich contexts,' I explored the development of expertise in teaching (Porath, 2009). This exploration emphasized the importance of understanding one's self as teacher as part of the process of becoming an educational virtuoso. I drew on Cohen's (2005) term, 'inner work' in thinking about this process, and I began to ponder more deeply just what the intrapersonal aspects of teaching involved and how they related to the very interpersonal world of teaching. How to represent the complex human undertaking that is teaching? Tracing its possible developmental course seemed only part of the picture.

Then—the invitation. An invitation is valued more or less for the context in which it is extended and by whom it is given. Who else is coming to the party? What's the occasion? What are the expectations? In this case, no such questions were asked. Avraham Cohen extended the invitation to become part of a group of like-minded colleagues who shared a deep commitment to education and an exceptionally thoughtful approach to their practice. We would engage in discussion of our own inner work and its role in our lives as educators. Already enriched by the conversations about the importance of inner work I had over tea with Avraham and knowing that the other invitees were colleagues I liked and respected, this was a most valued invitation.

Many of our initial meetings were held in the early morning over tea and scones at a congenial and artful teashop. All our gatherings and conversations are rich, humorous, and intellectually and personally satisfying, but my memories of the teashop meetings stand out. It was there that I grappled with the notion of inner work. Was I actually doing inner work? Was there a right way to do it? My world seemed, in some ways, so different from the worlds of other members of the group. But, at the same time, we shared a passion for the work of education and for thinking about it in insightful ways. And we had fun together—the perfect recipe for productive inner work.

Tea, scones, and conversation coincided with the time and space of a sabbatical that included the indulgence of a printmaking class. I was following a childhood love of art making that had, for too long, been lost in the business and busy-ness of academia. My colleagues' enthusiasm about that endeavour, their encouragement to share my work with them, and their responses to the images I created helped to nurture the realization that visual art is part of my inner world and my inner work. Finding and creating images that convey the artistry of teaching and thinking about teaching in artistic terms is essential both personally and professionally.

Turn the kaleidoscope. Fragments of shape and colour come together—again and again and again. There are many unified images. Image after image emerges, each one unique in its beauty. Each is right for thinking about inner work, educational challenges, educational insights, educational communities, educational creativity, love of teaching in certain ways at certain times. Each can facilitate realization of the essence of an attribute of teaching.
What is there in . . .
Negative spaces
   Intricate patterns
      Evocative textures
         Play of colour
Shadows
  Hues
Dancing light?

We bring who we are and what we love to education. We carry a palette and artist's tools with us—

Blending
    Toning
    Shading
Experimenting
Playing
    Viewing from different angles
    Critiquing
Allowing self to emerge/retreat/reemerge
Learning from each image we create
Celebrating others' palettes, the works they create, and the people they are.

> "No one saw flowers like Georgia O'Keeffe. No one saw people like Joan Miró" (Raczka, 2002, pp. 5, 12).

The arts have "artistic, disciplined, and imaginative qualities" (Cole & Knowles, 2008, p. 59) important to thinking about the complex world of education. They evoke empathy for others' ways of understanding and learning (Eisner, 2008) and bring new ways of understanding to students and teachers (Woo, 2008). Moreover, I would argue that when art is a part of a larger discussion about education and educators' inner lives and inner work it adds another dimension to thinking about and representing the work we do. It became woven into my colleagues' poetic, philosophical, Socratic, and living inquiry representations—mutually complementing the metaphors and analogies we derive to think about our practice. The artist's palette dances with poems, stories, contemplative walks on the beach, meditations on life. To paraphrase Alfred North Whitehead (as cited in Howe, 2006):

Ideas, facts, relationships, stories, histories, possibilities, artistry in words, in sounds, in form and in color, crowd into our lives, stir our feelings, excite our appreciation, and incite our impulses to kindred activities. (p. 132)

A kaleidoscope offers many coherent images.

REFERENCES

Cohen, A. (2005, April). Contemplations and rumours about the inner life of the educator: That which we are we shall teach. Paper presented at the American Educational Research Association, Montreal.

Cole, A. L., & Knowles, J. G. (2008). *Arts-informed research*. In J. G. Knowles & A. L. Cole (Eds.), Handbook of the arts in qualitative research (pp. 55-70). Los Angeles, CA: Sage.

Eisner, E. (2008). Art and knowledge. In J. G. Knowles & A. L. Cole (Eds.), *Handbook of the arts in qualitative research* (pp. 3–12). Los Angeles, CA: Sage.

Howe, R. (Ed.) (2006). *The quotable teacher*. Guilford, CT: The Lyons Press.

Porath, M. (2009). What makes a gifted educator? A design for development. In L. V. Shavinina (Ed.), *International handbook on giftedness* (pp. 825–838). New York: Springer.

Raczka, B. (2002). No one saw ordinary things through the eyes of an artist. Minneapolis, MN: Millbrook Press.

Woo, Y. Y. J. (2008). Engaging new audiences: Translating research into popular media. *Educational Researcher, 37*, 321–329.

With thanks to Shinsuke Minegushi and Lori Goldberg of Emily Carr University of Art + Design for their inspiration, creativity, innovative pedagogy, and belief that everyone is an artist.

DEVELOPING THE ARTISTRY OF TEACHING

I am privileged to be part of a group of educators who are exploring the place of inner work in our pedagogical practice. Different threads connect me to the members of the group—interests in the arts, creativity, and exceptional human accomplishments, dedication to students and to teaching, and longstanding respect. Our paths have converged in different ways, at different times, always with pleasure in the convergence. One shared belief is that inner work is different for all of us but especially for educators.

For me, the rediscovery of an ephemeral artistic self allowed me to ponder the relationships between art and my academic interests in cognitive developmental psychology and teaching. The things that interest me in developmental psychology are akin to art—my engagement with the things children do and say, the wonder of their logic, how they unite ideas and express them, how their ideas develop and change. Searching for the logic and creativity in thought is akin to determining composition and representing form. My curiosity about how the human mind develops, my wonder about the intellectual creativity involved in constructing new understandings and the unique ways in which individuals represent their understandings, and my love of seeing how intellectual growth happens are mirrored in my love of teaching and learning and the artistic forms in which I express myself. Unique patterns of growth in the curve of a stem, a delicately patterned leaf, blossoms opening, intertwining forms. One of my artistic explorations was to represent the complexities of teaching using the Celtic knot. The Celtic knot, as an art form, is believed to represent the intricacies of human existence. It is said that the "Celtic imagination loved the circle" (O'Donohue, 1997, p. xix)—the rhythm of experience is circular in nature. The work to which we aspire—articulating our inner work as educators—is also circular, intricate, complex.

Teaching is often characterized, at least in part, as an art—that indefinable something that brings curriculum, pedagogical strategies, and relationships with students to life and deepens their meaning.

Students to life and deepens their meaning. This artistry is often interpreted as the critical factor in moving beyond the 'how to' of teaching to a place where teachers are both inspired and inspiring, richly human in the way they interact with their understandings of what is taught and how, and with whom they co-construct learning.

> Every art, whether it be teaching, stone carving or judicial control of a court of law . . . has rules, but knowledge of the rules does not make one an artist. Art arises as the knower of the rules learns to apply them appropriately to the particular case. Application, in turn, requires acute awareness of the particularities of that case and ways in which the rule can be modified to fit the case without complete abrogation of the rule. In art, the form must be adapted to the matter. (Schwab, as cited in Shulman, 1986, p. 31)

Schwab's words bring some clarity to what artistry in teaching implies. However, how do we develop artistry in teaching? What allows the befriending of inner life and outer world of teaching? How does the "landscape of consciousness" (Bruner, 1986, p. x) about self and others as co-constructors of knowledge and members of a learning community evolve? How do we become sensitive to the variety of contexts in a classroom? Are there developmental precursors to this ability that can be noticed and nurtured? Are there steps along the way that need attention and support? How does a teacher who demonstrates such artistry maintain and evolve it?

> On a grey day in May in what now seems like a previous life, I sit in the Museum of Anthropology sketching. My grade four class is scattered about the museum engaged in observing and drawing the powerful images of the Northwest Coast First Nations people. I sit on a bench in a glass-enclosed enclave with a small boy at my side. Cedar trees bend and weave outside, embracing us, providing context for the cedar creature we are sketching. Jamie, a troubled and struggling student, and I sit, engrossed in recreating the image of a bear, trying to capture its life and power as rendered in cedar in two dimensions with pencil and paper. A magic moment in teaching—teacher and pupil lost to the world and totally absorbed in the wonder of coming to know and understand. Slowly I become aware that Jamie is saying something. "She's right here." I look up to see a woman smiling at me and realize she has asked Jamie where his teacher is. Jamie is looking slightly puzzled that she would ask this question. The woman is a staff member at the museum. She compliments me on the level of engagement of my students and their respect for the museum. "How wonderful," she says. "Such a

contrast to most school groups." I thank her and give credit to my students. Jamie is beaming.

Teaching satisfies,
nourishes, sustains me.
I'm proud of it.
It wasn't always like this.
A classic 'rough start'
Challenging contexts
Challenging students
What kept me going?

Moments of connection
Moments of laughter
Moments of sadness
Love of the work
Curiosity
Introspection
Try, and try again
Show care
Build trust
Connect the inner and outer worlds.

Inner work
   Sensing
      Expressions
      Body language
      Engagement
      Dynamics
   Questioning
      What lies behind their questions?
      Why?
      How are things understood?
      Why?

MARION PORATH

> What went before?
> Why? Why?
> Loving
> > Complexity
> > Seeing potential
> > Polishing
> > Creating
> > Learning

Have you ever really had a teacher? One who saw you as a raw but precious thing, a jewel that, with wisdom, could be polished to a proud shine? If you are lucky enough to find your way to such teachers, you will always find your way back. (Albom, 1997, p. 192)

More and more, I tried to capture the imagery of the interconnections in teaching. There was this vague but beautiful sensation—a silvery haze but no discernible images. How to represent the artistry of teaching? Words were not enough.

> Dialectical
> > Hierarchical
> > > Spiral
> > > > Complex
> > > > Integrated
> > > > > An interplay of minds
> > > > > Mindful interplay
> > > > > Mindful play

Jewels in the crown
   Teachers polish.

So do students when they learn in a place where work is the poetics of growth (O'Donohue, 1997). Each student contributes to their own growth and others' shine so that, in the end, they demonstrate and feel a well-crafted competence that is part of a larger demonstration of competence, a contribution to an achievement where the whole is greater than the sum of its parts. This is the artistry.

So –

How *does* one become sensitive to the variety of contexts in a classroom? Are there developmental precursors to this ability that can be noticed and nurtured? Are there steps along the way that need attention and support? How does a teacher who demonstrates such artistry maintain it and continue to evolve? From my perspective as an educational psychologist, there are some clues in the educational and developmental psychological literature that suggest that ability as an educator is better understood not as "in the head" of the teacher (Barab & Plucker, 2002, p. 166) but rather as situated in context. Teachers and teaching, then, are understood in the complex contexts of educational environments, with acknowledgment of the reciprocal influences of educational environment and teacher-student connectedness. However, the heart of the teacher must be part of this understanding.

We come closer to capturing the heart of pedagogy in Arlin's (1999) articulation of the wise teacher as one who reflects "an orientation toward self, students, and teaching that highlights the teacher as learner in the act of constructing knowledge with her students" (p. 12). Wisdom is a profound developmental phenomenon that encompasses understanding of and interest in the nature of knowledge, ambiguity, and others' minds and the contexts in which learning unfolds (Arlin, 1999). Heart and the relationship between the educator's inner and outer worlds are captured in her description of wise teachers as those who "have the humility and courage to live with uncertainty and take the risk of questioning whether they can do better" (Arlin, 1999, p. 16).

As a young, highly intelligent child once told me, wise is not the same as smart (Porath, 1997). She was correct—intelligence and wisdom are not the same (Baltes & Staudinger, 2000). It is the interplay of intelligence and one's openness to experience, personal growth, and 'psychological mindedness' and what results in this interplay (creativity, cognitive style, and social intelligence) that are the ingredients of wisdom. On the other hand, a commonly held belief that older means wiser is incorrect; experience matters only when it interacts with intelligence and openness to experience, commitment to personal growth, and a psychological mindset (Baltes & Staudinger, 2000).

Gardner (1983) described 'gifted teachers' as demonstrating highly developed interpersonal, or social, intelligence. Together with its 'companion,' intrapersonal intelligence (Gardner, 1993), the 'personal intelligences' offer additional possibilities for thinking about what inner work entails. Intrapersonal intelligence turns inward the abilities of the interpersonally intelligent to read the intentions and desires of others and to act upon this knowledge. Gardner (1983) described the core capacity of intrapersonal intelligence as "access to one's own feeling life" (p. 239). In its most advanced form, "intrapersonal knowledge allows one to detect and to symbolize complex and highly differentiated sets of feelings" (Gardner, 1983, p. 239). A noteworthy educator may, then, use his or her own depth of knowledge of self in relating to, supporting, and understanding students. Arlin (1999) too, incorporated "orientation toward self" (p. 12) in her definition of a wise teacher. Wise teachers see themselves as co-learners with their students, thus blending interpersonal (teacher) and intrapersonal (learner) constructions of self. They are comfortable with the risks and challenges inherent in uncovering diverse points of view. Teaching does, in fact, demand "a heavy investment of the self" (Turner-Bisset, 1999, p. 46).

Latour's (1999) notions about shifting frames of reference are helpful in capturing what likely happens in noteworthy teaching. Such educators may relate different, unrelated frames of reference to one another, "shifting out" (p. 129) from one to another, juxtaposing the two, and "shifting down" (p. 189) when a completely new frame of reference is evident. These shifts result in a "depth of vision" (p. 311). Using another artistic analogy, teaching in this way might be described as orchestration at the virtuoso level (Porath, 2009), and may develop in the following way. Psychological profiles of students and self are integrated, understood as shifting frames of reference, and coordinated with one's pedagogical content knowledge. Knowledge of what is taught, how it is taught, and the complex human beings with whom one interacts is effectively coordinated in one's pedagogy. As one develops further in one's ability to orchestrate pedagogy, relativistic knowledge of students and self is related to pedagogical content knowledge and knowledge of the developmental structure of the discipline. Finally, the changing landscape of relativistic thought as related to pedagogical content knowledge and knowledge of the developmental structure of the discipline is understood in the social-cultural context.

Virtuosity needs nurturance. How do we get to this depth of vision? The question has important implications for teacher education. If one is committed to "work as a poetics of growth" (O'Donohue, 1997, p. xix)—an artistic blend of one's outer world as an educator and one's inner life and the awakening of a new imagination (O'Donohue, 1997)—then it is clearly important to support beginning teachers in this quest. They are likely to enter teacher education with varying abilities to reflect on their inner lives and the meaning of those lives to their work as educators. A 'roadmap' of what development might entail may assist them in their journeys to deeper visions of pedagogy. Such a map could guide teacher educators in supporting beginning teachers to practice in a way that is rewarding for them. It should be noted, though, that such a map should not be used in a rigid way. Beginning teachers may begin and end in different places, take alternate routes, and make interesting detours.

A DEVELOPMENTAL ROAD MAP TO ARTISTRY IN TEACHING

While speculative, the following is offered as a developmental road map (Porath, 2009). Beginning teachers may be in a place where they do not reflect on their inner selves in relation to their work as teachers. They may view teaching simply as a series of actions or tasks to be accomplished. They could be supported in gradually integrating *dimensions of themselves* into their professional work, first by recognizing relationships of single emotions to teaching tasks. Once that integration is consolidated, they could move to relating two or more emotions to different teaching tasks and then to integration of emotions and teaching tasks with a social or moral judgment or social-educational rule. At this stage, judgments and rules may be articulated in a rote way without consideration of the consequences for not following rules. Beginning teachers may need to be supported in thinking about different frames of reference regarding judgments and rules. Theoretically, this should lead to realization of a more interpretive view of self. [Action-based, dimensional, and *interpretive descriptions of self-understanding* were adapted from Malcolm (2005)].

An interpretive stance may imply that understandings and insights about one's self are generalized to different situations and that consequences of not following a social rule or judgment are recognized. Gradually, enhanced self-understanding is achieved as one questions one's own beliefs and values and one's beliefs about teaching and learning become more abstract. Questions about beliefs and values simply 'are'—they do not need resolution.

Continued inner work can lead to a firm identity of self as teacher, a teacher who can detect and symbolize complex and highly differentiated sets of feelings (Gardner, 1983) as they relate to elaborated beliefs and values about teaching. Complex feelings, beliefs, and values provide the basis for inner work related to teaching. Depth of knowledge resulting from inner work, however that is conceived, is used in relating to, supporting, and understanding students. Important in this notion of development as a teacher, though, is the notion of shoshin, which, in Japanese means beginner's mind (Davey, 2007)—a "consciousness that's always fresh, never bogged down by its own past" (Davey, 2007, p. 47). Without shoshin, we cease to learn; with it, we see our teaching as continually new, always growing and developing as educators. "Every instant is ultimately different, and art, beauty, and success must be found right in that instant or it will not take place" (Davey, 2007, p. 47).

Our group has supported our collective and individual journeys toward understanding our inner work as teachers. We think there may be a connection between one's inner work and successful teaching. We're still exploring. Rich ideas, rich representations of those ideas, the sharing of stories and explorations of what led us to teaching, provocative questions, humour, good food, and tea have sustained us and made us eager for more.

We shall not cease from exploration
And the end of all our exploring
Will be to arrive where we started
And know the place for the first time.
(Eliot, 1925/1936/1963, p. 209)

REFERENCES

Albom, M. (1997). *Tuesdays with Morrie. An old man, a young man, and life's greatest lesson.* New York: Doubleday.
Arlin, P. K. (1999). The wise teacher: A developmental model of teaching. *Theory into Practice, 38,* 12-17.
Baltes, P. B., & Staudinger, U. M. (2000). Wisdom: A metaheuristic (pragmatic) to orchestrate mind and virtue toward excellence. *American Psychologist, 55,* 122–136.
Barab, S. A., & Plucker, J. A. (2002). Smart people or smart contexts? Cognition, ability, and talent development in an age of situated approaches to knowing and learning. *Educational Psychologist, 37,* 165-182.
Bruner, J. (1986). *Actual minds, possible worlds.* Cambridge, MA: Harvard University Press.
Davey, H. E. (2007). *The Japanese way of the artist.* Berkeley, CA: Stone Bridge Press.
Eliot, T. S. (1925/1936/1963). *Collected poems 1909-1962.* London, England: faber and faber.
Gardner, H. (1983). *Frames of mind: The theory of multiple intelligences.* New York: Basic Books.
Gardner, H. (1993). Multiple intelligences: The theory in practice. New York: Basic Books.
Latour, R. (1999). *Pandora's hope: Essays on the reality of science studies.* Cambridge, MA: Harvard University Press.

Malcolm, J. (2005). *A developmental analysis of adolescents' life stories: Narrative coherence and meaning-making.* Unpublished doctoral dissertation, University of Calgary.

O'Donohue, J. (1997). *Anam čara: A book of Celtic wisdom.* New York: HarperCollins.

Porath, M. (1997). Gifted children's understanding of intelligence. *Roeper Review, 20,* 95–98.

Porath, M. (2009). What makes a gifted educator? A design for development. In L. V. Shavinina (Ed.), *International handbook on giftedness* (pp. 825-838). New York: Springer.

Shulman, L. S. (1986). Paradigms and research programs in the study of teaching: A contemporary perspective. In M. C. Wittrock (Ed.), *Handbook of research on teaching* (3rd ed.). (pp. 3-36). New York: MacMillan.

Turner-Bisset, R. (1999). The knowledge bases of the expert teacher. *British Educational Research Journal, 25,* 39–55.

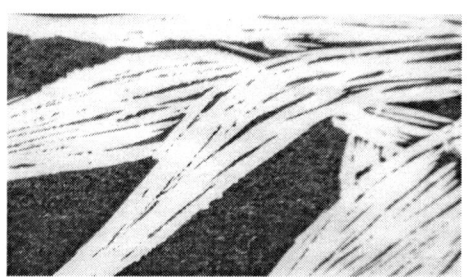

INNERWORKINGS

ANTHONY CLARKE

ATTENDING TO THE WORLD DIFFERENTLY

Someone once said I was a distraction . . .

DISTRACTIONS

How would you describe your life?

> Someone once said I was a distraction.

A distraction?

> Yes.

That's a bit harsh. Most people would like to be a Main Event rather than a distraction.

> Yes, I suppose so.

So, would you like to be a Main Event?

> People line up for a long time, pay big money, and get dressed up for a Main Event!

And?

> You don't do that for a distraction.

Oh. Why?

> Because you can't anticipate a distraction. If you did, it wouldn't be a distraction.

Is that good or bad?

> It all depends.

How do you mean?

> Some people are highly focused and see distractions as bothersome; they deliberately school themselves against being distracted.

So that's a good thing?

> I guess. For some people.

But?

> It might be different for other people.

ATTENDING TO THE WORLD DIFFERENTLY

Meaning?

> Isaac Newton was distracted all the time but he noticed things that other people didn't—an apple falling from a tree. Woody Allen is always getting distracted and is good at noticing things that others don't—90% of life is just showing up. Leonard Cohen. Now there is someone who gets distracted and, as a result, sees things that others miss—there is a crack in everything/that is how the light gets in.

I once heard about someone who noticed pedagogy in the most unusual places.

> Hmmm.

Yeah, pretty weird!

> So, do you get distracted?

No. Yes. No. Well, sometimes. Nobody has asked me that question before. I guess it is a bit like the time my English teacher sent me out of the classroom and made me stand in the corridor for not paying attention.

> Hmmm.

But I *was* paying attention but not to what he thought I should be paying attention to. So, I got sent out. You know, sometimes distractions are important; you have to pay attention to them.

> Ah, ha.

And because I got sent out of class I was able to concentrate on what was distracting me.

Ah, ha.

So I guess that sometimes a distraction might be a good thing.

> Hmmm.

Like grandchildren. Boy, are they ever distracting!

> Hmmm.

And aesthetic moments; that deep resonance within that catches you unaware. Have you ever felt that?

> Yes, I think so.

And silence. A rare thing these days but when it happens, it surprises us.

    Ah, ha.

And falling in love. The ultimate distraction.

    Ah.

What do you call it when things happen that you don't plan for?

    Um?

Serendipity. That's it.

    Yes.

Wow. Where did that all that come from? Somewhere inside. Huh!

    Inside?

Wait a minute! I'm the one who is supposed to be asking the questions. Are you trying to *distract* me?

> *There is no such thing as a 'distraction.'*
> *If you notice something, it is speaking to you.*
> *And then, it is the 'listening' that becomes important.*

BURGEO AND BACK!

OR

Living Pedagogically: Catching Oneself in the Act of Being Attentive to Pedagogy

BURGEO

I moved from my hometown in Melbourne, Australia, where I had been a high school teacher for 11 years, to attend the University of British Columbia, Vancouver, Canada. Graduate school was only one reason for my move to Canada. I also enjoy the outdoors and Canada's west coast is well known as an outdoor enthusiast's playground. When not studying, I spent many hours cycling, sailing, kayaking, and hiking Canada's Pacific northwest. In 1992 an opportunity to visit eastern Canada arose and with it my first opportunity to explore the Atlantic provinces. The national research conference in education—Canadian Society for the Study of Education (CSSE)—was in Prince Edward Island (PEl), 12 kilometers off mainland Canada in the Atlantic Ocean. The neighbouring provinces of Nova Scotia, connected by a land bridge to the mainland, and Newfoundland, an island to the north of PEl, also beckoned. I flew east, attended the conference, and then set out to explore PEl, Nova Scotia, and Newfoundland by bike.

It was mid-June, a couple of weeks before the beginning of summer, so the roads and campgrounds were virtually empty. (I was not entirely alone as the sand flies on the famous Cabot Trail were particularly friendly.) After cycling around PEl and Nova Scotia, I caught a ferry from Sydney, Nova Scotia, to Port Aux Basques in Newfoundland. It was a six-hour journey and I arrived late in the evening. Early the next morning, I boarded a small passenger ferry (capacity 35 people) and made my way along the southern coast of Newfoundland. Newfoundland is known as 'the Rock' and many of the coastal communities—known as outport towns—cling precariously to the rugged shoreline and are only accessible by water. By mid-afternoon, the ferry arrived at Burgeo, 100 kilometres from Port Aux Basques—see the illustration below.

ANTHONY CLARKE

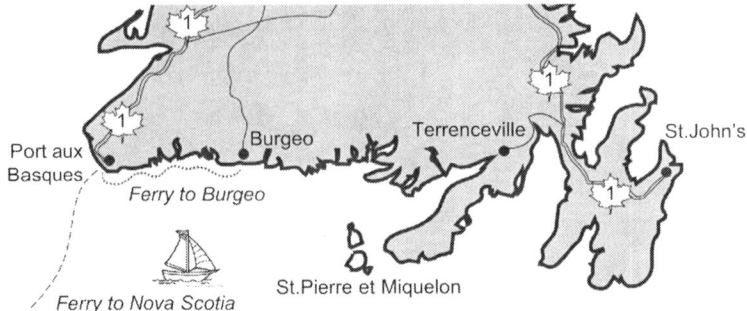

Newfoundland - Southern coast

Burgeo is one of the more substantial communities on the southern coast and has a road connecting it to the rest of the province. By road, Burgeo is 300 kilometres from Port-Aux-Basques. As you sail into the Burgeo harbour you are greeted by a beautiful sandy beach to the left of the town. The beach and surrounding area is part of Sandbanks Provincial Park. The park has 25 campsites and was one of the reasons for my visit to this remote community.

Cycling down the wharf and slowly through the small town, I am greeted by friendly smiles and the occasional wave from the locals. I sense a strong feeling of pride and history that the town's people have for their community. A left turn at the end of the main street and a short ride along a narrow road brings me to the Sandbanks Provincial Park. I introduce myself to the park ranger. We chat briefly. He is a long time employee of Parks Canada and his main task in the coming weeks is to prepare the park for the holiday season. He tells me that I am the only visitor in the park and, as such, I have 'the pick of the campsites.' I pay my camping fee, find a beautiful campsite and pitch my tent. Later, I wander into town and have dinner at a small restaurant (a treat for a touring cyclist!). I return to my tent and am lulled to sleep by the sound of waves caressing the sandy shoreline. The next morning I explore the 12 kilometres of trails (including beaches, rocky headlands, sandspit formations, and grasslands). I return in the early afternoon and decide to take it easy (the ferry only runs every other day) and with a book in hand I sit down to enjoy the warmth of the afternoon sunshine. A short time later, I hear a vehicle heading my way. I glance around to see the park ranger, accompanied by a second ranger, driving a tractor with a trailer. They stop about five campsites away. As they begin to work their 'background' conversation floats in and out of my consciousness.

The following day I board the ferry to Terrenceville and from there ride my bike overland to St. John's, the capital city of Newfoundland. More adventures are in store: unexpectedly overnighting in a bus shelter in Terrenceville, being overrun by a girl guide troop in Pippy Park, etc.

However, my visit to Burgeo was to become one of the most memorable experiences of my trip to Atlantic Canada. Why? There are many interesting events to recount about Burgeo. While hiking along the grasslands immediately above the beach, I came across the First Settlers graveyard, extraordinary not only for its age but for the image it evokes of early settler life in such a remote part of the world. I also found the people of Burgeo to be truly wonderful and the hospitality they offer to visitors is exceptional. The unique coastal lifestyle is a delight; nothing is so important that cannot be interrupted to spend a moment (or longer) with friends and strangers alike. There is a palpable sense of community in Burgeo that I rarely experience in larger towns or cities.

BURGEO AND BACK!

It was only much later after my return to Vancouver that I realized that my memories of Burgeo were not so much about the beauty of the park, the friendliness of the people, or the sense of community, but were focused more on a peripheral event that had lodged itself firmly in my subconscious. When recounting my visit to Burgeo I started the story in much the same way as described above—a coastal ferry trip, a beautiful beach, and a campground all to myself—but my retelling then takes an unexpected turn:

As I read my book I find myself increasingly attending to the conversation and activities of the two park rangers. It becomes apparent that the second ranger, a young woman, is a university student working for Parks Canada as a summer job. As I catch snippets of their conversation, it is clear that the senior ranger is knowledgeable and experienced and the new ranger is keen to learn as much as possible about her job. The rangers are bringing one of the 'portable' toilets out of winter storage and assembling it in preparation for the summer season. They go about their work in an unhurried manner and their interaction is courteous and respectful. The senior ranger explains the various items to be used: spanners, wooden runners, nuts, bolts, crowbars, etc. They inspect the site and he suggests a possible way to go about the task based on previous experience. At all times, he is conscious of asking the young woman if she has any questions and allows opportunities for her to provide suggestions. First they have to remove the cover plate that was installed over the site at the end of previous summer. With the assistance of the new park ranger, the senior ranger reverses the trailer into a position in line with the site. After a short discussion, the two of them slide the toilet off the back of the trailer and into an upright position. Working from either side of the toilet and using wooden runners they nudge the toilet into place with crowbars. Next, using the crowbars as levers they remove the runners. After further adjustments they secure the toilet in place with bolts. They then attach the door and attend to a range of other tasks necessary for completion of the job. The process takes about two hours from start to finish.

So what piqued my curiosity about two park rangers assembling a toilet in the middle of nowhere[2]? This event is hardly something worth remembering, let alone retelling.

---

[2] My apologies to Burgeo. It is its remoteness that makes it such an extraordinary place!

I recall thinking at the time that it would have been a lot quicker if the senior ranger had assembled the toilet himself, and only called on the 'extra hand' when required (e.g., sliding the toilet off the trailer). He clearly had the knowledge and experience to do the whole task almost unaided; the toilet structure was relatively light as the internal frame and external panels were made of aluminum. Stopping frequently and explaining the details associated with assembling the toilet seemed largely unnecessary and very time consuming. It wasn't as if he was required to assemble a bank of toilets and that teaching the new park ranger to assemble the first would free him to do other things while she assembled the remainder. However, he did not treat the new ranger as just an 'extra hand.' Rather, he treated her as part of 'the team.' He made sure that she felt integral to the work that they were doing. He treated her with respect and courtesy. He did not 'speak down' to her. He did not dismiss her contribution just because she was a beginning park ranger. I recall thinking that if I were the parent of the young woman and had heard about her summer job as a park ranger I might have expected her to be assigned to menial tasks and not engaged in day-to-day work of a real park ranger—or in the words of Lave and Wegner (1991) "the mature practices of the community" (p. 109). After observing the interaction between the two rangers I don't think that I could imagine a better working relationship between an experienced veteran and a new employee of Parks Canada. She was treated as an important member of the ranger community and she was being thoughtfully and deliberately schooled in the ways of being a park ranger.

After retelling my Burgeo story a number of times, and more recently to Avraham and our group, I began to realize how attentive I had been to the pedagogy that unfolded in the interaction between the two rangers. It seems that whenever I am in a situation where someone is explaining or demonstrating something to someone else, I can't help but ask myself: Would I do it the same way? Use the same explanation? Approach? Why? Why not? I expect this internal conversation to occur when I am in a regular teaching/learning context where the raison d'etre is explicitly pedagogic (e.g., an elementary classroom, a secondary school auditorium, or a university lecture theatre). What surprises me, however, is the variety of out-of-school contexts in which I catch myself being attentive to pedagogy.

LIVING PEDAGOGICALLY

The genesis of this paper arises from Avraham Cohen's curiosity about the 'inner life of the educator.' For Avraham, attending to one's inner life is about a consciousness of being in the world. Avraham has explored this concept in his own research and teaching (Cohen, 2009). As a result of these endeavours, he began to wonder if there might be an important connection between attending to one's inner life as an educator and one's success as a teacher. Based on a review of the teaching and learning literature, Avraham concluded that the inner life of the educator had been largely ignored in education. As a practicing psychotherapist, this seemed to be an anomaly to Avraham, particularly when a teacher's sense of professional efficacy and classroom success is in important ways tied to his or her sense of self as teacher (Kagan, 1992).

Avraham reasoned that if there was a connection between attending to one's inner life as an educator and successful teaching, then a good starting point would be to talk to teachers whose peers and pupils regarded them as exemplary. Therefore, he decided to bring together a group of 'award winning educators' (his phrase) and engage them in a series of conversations about their teaching hoping in the process to gain some insight into if and how they attended to their inner lives as educators. I was fortunate to be invited to join the group.

When we first met I had no idea of where this inquiry would lead nor did I have any real sense of how I would inquire into the notion of my inner life as an educator. In the early meetings, I quickly formed the opinion that attending to one's inner life probably meant spending time in meditation—a practice that Avraham engaged in each day and about which I knew little prior to listening to Avraham describe the importance of this practice for him. It also seemed that other members of the group were similarly at a loss when it came to thinking about their inner life and the role it might play in their success as educators. However, we knew and respected Avraham and, if nothing else, the invitation to meet as a group was an opportunity to enjoy each other's company, something that did not happen often in our professional lives. Therefore, we were prepared to hold in abeyance our doubts and reservations about Avraham's inquiry and agreed to meet with an open mind as to what might emerge.

From the very first meeting it was clear that we were all committed to teaching, one of the three professional expectations of university educators; research and service being the other two. It seemed that we all spent a great deal of time in planning and providing the best possible learning environment for our students. Further, we seemed to seek out professional development opportunities that would contribute to the improvement of our teaching whenever possible. When it came to thinking about our inner lives, other than Avraham and one other member of the group, it was apparent that we did not consciously spend much time doing this and certainly not in the way that most of us conceived of this concept at the outset of the inquiry. It seemed to me that this 'neglect' was even more apparent when questioned about the time we spent thinking about our inner lives as educators. Indeed, we struggled to even describe what the phrase 'inner life' meant and often looked to Avraham to explain it to us—however Avraham would provide, at most, a very general description and then re-direct the question to the group for further discussion.

About midway through the first year of our meetings, we thought that a presentation at a conference might be a useful way to focus our discussions. We chose a conference and worked collectively on a proposal submission. Choosing a title for our proposal became important because it would signal to the conference delegates the enterprise that we were engaged in. There were many suggestions and finally we chose the phrase 'Living Pedagogically' as the overarching theme because we thought it best captured the nature and substance of our conversations. Living pedagogically suggests that teaching, as a professional practice, is not something that you take up when you arrive at the school entrance and then leave there when you depart at the end of the school day. Rather, teaching is something that is deeply embedded in and becomes part of the way in which you make sense of, negotiate, and give shape to your life both within and beyond the classroom. It would be hard to imagine living the contradiction whereby in one part of your life you are conscious of and curious about pedagogy, and in another part of your life you ignore it entirely (e.g., when playing with children, working with youth, organizing a community event, etc.).

INNER WORK?

Over the course of our meetings, Avraham's notion of 'inner life' was being reshaped through our collective engagement and the outcome was the adoption of inner work as a more accessible, and possibly more generative, way of thinking about living pedagogically. Where inner life seemed to be something deeply internal, almost monastic in its meditative and contemplative undertones, inner work seemed to be more active in its orientation and had an immediacy that allowed the group to think in more tangible ways about living pedagogically. As a result, the conversation took on a more lively and animated character with each of us sharing individually and responding collectively to the ways in which our outward engagement with the world might interact with our inner lives as educators. For my own part, I continued to wonder if I actually engaged in any inner work at all, and if so, what form it took. Fortunately, there seemed to be no limit to the ways in which our conversations with Avraham unfolded. These exchanges were truly Gadamarian (1990) in nature:

> We say that we "conduct" a conversation, but the more genuine a conversation is, the less its conduct lies within the will of either partner. Thus a genuine conversation is never the one that we wanted to conduct. Rather, it is generally more correct to say that we fall into conversation, or even that we become involved in it. The way one word follows another, with the conversation taking its own twists and reaching its own conclusion, may well be conducted in some way, but the partners conversing are far less the leaders of it than the led. No one knows in advance what will "come out" of a conversation. (pp. 383-384)

While our conversations may have seemed unruly at times, a degree of individual convergence emerged for each of us in the way we potentially engaged in inner work. For some, our discussions revealed the importance of creative writing as a vehicle for enabling this. For others it was meditation. For others it was performative endeavours. I was surprised to find that my contributions to the conversation seemed to converge around the idea that I tend to be curious about pedagogy in the most unusual places, something I didn't know prior to joining Avraham's group. The Burgeo story is one example. Other stories with a similar theme included my year seven pupils' interactions with a farmer during a school camp and my gymnastic team's response to a performance by Marcel Marceau.

Might catching myself in the act of being attentive to pedagogy be a form of inner work? As I reflected further on my stories, I realized that catching myself in the act of being attentive to pedagogy did not, in and of itself, constitute inner work, but it seemed to be an important first step. This realization moved my inquiry forward in important ways. I now found myself asking: What is the nature of inner work that is occasioned by catching myself in the act of being attentive to pedagogy? In responding to this question, it became apparent that while being attentive is important, it is the act of remembering and retelling that is of greater significance for the inner work that I (possibly) engage in as an educator.

A RENDERING OF THE OTHER IS ALWAYS AT SOME LEVEL A RENDERING OF SELF

Remembering or retelling requires selective attention. In any situation, there will always be many more details to report than we can possibly capture or share regardless of the comprehensiveness of the method or medium available for us to do so. When we notice something (either consciously or unconsciously) we attend to a set of particulars. These particulars are shaped by numerous factors, none the least of which is our world view (De Witt, 2004). Each of us attends to particulars differently and sometimes to a different set of particulars altogether for the same event. Further, no individual (or collective) remembering or retelling can ever render accurately the original event.

The process of remembering and retelling draws upon various capacities, a process akin to Schön's (1987) notion of framing and reframing. In remembering and retelling I identify, problematize, and specify what it is that I am being attentive to. As I do this, I also draw on my feelings and emotions in re-storying the event. I set the stage and paint the landscape to sufficiently portray as vividly as possible the essence of the event as it unfolded for me. I give emphasis to some elements and relegate others to background colour. Each of these decisions requires that I pause, think, and then act—that is, to make choices.

As I relate my Burgeo story I inhabit the minds of the two actors. I intuit and give reason to their respective actions in the retelling. As such, my particular rendering of the interaction between the park rangers is a generative reconstruction of a vicariously lived pedagogical event. Unavoidably, I am deeply implicated in the retelling. The story and 'I' are interwoven and although the difference between the two might not be readily apparent, if you listen carefully, I reveal as much about myself as I do about the two park rangers. The rendering of 'the other' is a rendering of 'self'—of myself. I am forever changed by the remembering and retelling. As I write 'the text' I am written by 'the text.'

A CONSCIOUSNESS OF BEING IN THE WORLD

If, as Avraham suggests, that inner work has the potential for increasing our consciousness of being in the world, and a greater consciousness enhances the ways in which we relate to the people and contexts in which we live and work, how might catching myself being attentive to pedagogy enhance my teaching practice? As noted above, I realized that being attentive to pedagogy alone did not, in and of itself, constitute inner work. It is the remembering and retelling that provides for a rendering of the relationship between teacher and learner. In retelling my Burgeo experience, I reveal my beliefs and sensibilities about pedagogical practice, paying attention to both the particular (as revealed in the details I give emphasis to) and the general (as revealed in the underlying message that I convey about the relationship). This 'one-step removed' narrative of 'the other' (in this instance, the pedagogical relationship between the two rangers) provides a safe distance for thinking more deeply about my own practice. Rendering 'the other' allows me to be attentive to and articulate the pedagogical moment of Burgeo in a way that is not always possible in the real time moments of my own pedagogical practice but in a way, nonetheless, that foregrounds my taken-for-granted assumptions about pedagogy. Thus, I would argue that a rendering of self, in whatever shape it might take (in my case, catching myself being attentive to pedagogy), constitutes inner work. Further, catching myself being attentive to pedagogy and then remembering and retelling allows for the generative potential of that work. As Edelman (2000) reminds us: "Every act of perception, is to some degree an act of creation, and every act of memory is to some degree an act of imagination" (p. 56). The critical point here is that inner work is a creative act. Some of the other ways that inner work might be undertaken are revealed by the members of Avraham's group: poetry, art, living inquiry, meditation, and so on. Each draws on contemplative traditions (Duerr, 2004) in some way, shape, or form. All have the potential for enabling us to be conscious of being in the world. As such, inner work nourishes, sustains, and energizes our lives and our professional practices.

REFERENCES

Cohen, A. (2009). *Gateway to the Dao-Field: Essays for the Awakening Educator*. Cambria

Drevdahl, D. J., Stackman, R. W., Purdy, J. M., & Louie, B. Y. (2002). Merging reflective inquiry and self-study as a framework for enhancing the scholarship of teaching. *Journal of Nursing Education, 41*(9), 413–419.

Duerr, M. (2004). *A powerful silence: The role of meditation and other contemplative practices in American life and work*. Northampton, MA: Center for Contemplative Mind in Society.

DeWitt, R. (2004). *Worldviews: An introduction to the history and philosophy of science*. Blackwell Publishing.

Edelman, G. (2000). *The brain*. London (UK): Transaction Publishers.

Gadamer, H.G. (1990). *Truth and method* (2nd ed.) (J. Weinsheimer & D. Marshall, Trans.). New York: Crossroad. (Original work published 1960)

Kagan, D. (1992). Professional Growth Among Pre service and Beginning *Teachers. Review of Educational Research, 62*(2), 129–169.

Lave, J., & Wenger, E. (1991) *Situated learning: Legitimate peripheral participation*. Cambridge: Cambridge University Press.

Schön, D. (1987). *Educating the Reflective Practitioner*. San Francisco: Jossey-Bass.

INNERWORKINGS

HEESOON BAI

EDUCATION FOR ENLIGHTENMENT

I have been a student of Buddha most of my adult life—for over 30 years now . . .

ACADEMIC SANGHA

Experiment in Being Here-and-Now

I have been a student of Buddha most of my adult life—for over 30 years now. And it does not look like I will graduate from this course of study. No degree, no certificate. Not only that, I am not even sure if I will ever achieve the goal of this study: enlightenment. In fact, if I understand the Buddha's teachings correctly, enlightenment is not something one can achieve by effort as this very striving and achieving drive will guarantee failure. Paradox abounds. What do humans do in the face of paradox and failure? We try to run forward and backward, in time, in space, or in logic, we run away and run around crazily, but in the end, we just sit down, exhausted. It turns out that's what zazen (just sitting) is essentially about. We just sit and face who I am, how I am, and what's happening in my consciousness as I look out at the world. Chödrön (1991), contemporary teacher in the tradition of Shambhala Buddhism, states:

> One of the main discoveries of meditation is seeing how we continually run away from the present moment, how we avoid being here just as we are. That's not considered to be a problem; the point is to see it. (p. 3)

Where does this inability to be in the here-and-now come from? If life exists only in the here-and-now, and we have this inability, then logic dictates that we don't really live. A distressing thought! A French philosopher living some 300 years earlier than Chödrön registered exactly the same distress, and expressed it with his usual penetrating insight and precision. His name is Pascal (1623–1662), and he left the following entry in his Pensées (1966):

> We never keep to the present . . . We are so unwise that we wander about in times that do not belong to us, and do not think of the only one that does; so vain that we dream of times that are not and blindly flee the only one that is. The fact is that the present usually hurts. We thrust it out of sight because it distresses us, and if we find it enjoyable, we are sorry it slips away. We try to give it the support of the future, and think how we are going to arrange things over which we have no control for a time we can never be sure of reaching . . . The present is never our end. The past and the present are our means, the future alone our end. Thus we never actually live, but hope to live, and since we are always planning how to be happy, it is inevitable that we should never be so. (p. 43)

I ask again: where does this inability to be in the here-and-now come from? I do not know its origin, but I do know, from my own schooling experience as well as my current professorial work as professor in Education, that the way we educate people—in content, values, aims, and manner—does not do a good job of developing the ability to be in the here-and-now. How could it, when our education is mostly, if not all, about the future—future survival, success, achievement, improvement, and—a favourite buzz word in education today—transformation? We are consumed by future achievement and success, and the cultural logic behind this future orientation is individual survival. Parents everywhere repeat variations of 'If you don't study and work hard, you will be pushing a shopping cart!' Some variations are, I am sure, more gentle and kind than others: all the same, they voice fear and insecurity about the future.

All my life I knew best how to study hard, compete, win and survive. I survived the so-called 'Examination Hell' in Korea—12 long years of enforced studying, under constant fear of failure. After I immigrated to Canada at the age of 17, I basically did the same: studied single-mindedly, while struggling with learning English, and obtained a bachelor's degree in Honours Philosophy with the Gold Medal. Certainly, this is the way of worldly achievement, but life cannot be sustained through such achievement only. As Pascal (1966) reminded us, if we don't live here-and-now, in an important way, we don't live at all. Hence, meditation practice became an important corrective or balance to my life when I came to understand that meditation is all about being open to the here-and-now. Meditation is about being in touch with each emergent moment; fully experiencing it and being fully present. Meditation is not interested in what we can do better or change for the better—in the future and for the future. In meditation, everything is brought to the present—to this moment. What is happening this moment? What am I experiencing, seeing this moment? How am I disposed to the world this moment? How am I relating to people this moment? To truly see, with precision, what is happening in each moment, we need to be wide awake and wide open, full of curiosity, gentleness, and compassion. As Pascal indicated, the present moment usually hurts, and we usually don't want to face it. To face the present moment with its existential and material hurts, discomforts, distress, and disappointment, we need a lot of equanimity and compassion—towards our selves and others. If I can live each moment with equanimity and compassion, wisdom of love and love of wisdom, I am ready for life, come what may.

I started out as a solitary meditator, and I still meditate alone regularly. Over the years, in increasingly infusing meditation into my pedagogy and classroom learning experience, I have come to see meditation not so much as an activity but rather as an attribute of who we are as relational beings: wide awake, wide open, compassionate, gentle and kind, and care-full. As such, meditation is a way of being and way of life, and there is no better place to practice it than in the company of each other. The Innerworking Educators' group that came together under the leadership of Avraham Cohen turned out to be the right company for my ever-present beginning level of equanimity and compassion. With these colleagues, my heart naturally and easily opens wide; and my intellect comes alive during our lively and joyful dialogue. My whole being resonates deeply with the generosity of their heart and spirit. I would not hesitate to call my manner of being with them an active meditation. As my sitting meditation nourishes me, a morning or an afternoon in the company of my colleagues (whose work you read in these chapters) replenishes me, deeply. Knowing that these colleagues are in the academy gives me hope, comfort, and a sense of solidarity.

REFERENCES

Chödrön, P. (1991). The wisdom of no escape and the path of loving-kindness. Boston: Shambhala Publications.

Pascal, B. (1966). *Pensées*, A. J. Krailsheimer (Ed. & Trans.) London: Penguin Books.

ENTERING THE FIELD OF BEING

Inner Work and Education for Enlightenment

Teaching necessarily happens in the intersection of the personal and the professional. The more integration we can achieve between these two realms, the more embodied, enactive, and alive our teaching becomes, which, in turn, can facilitate transformative learning in our students. This integration of the personal and the professional is supported by what our group calls the innerworkings for educators.

We tend to think and act in terms of such dichotomies as private/public, subjective/objective, emotional/rational, senses/intellect, making integration of the personal (where the first terms reside) with the professional (where the second terms reside) challenging work. For a lot of professionals, including teachers, this dichotomy means concealing many dimensions of the personal from our professional context. A prime example is the substantial exclusion of our rich emotional lives and resources that might be related to how we make decisions and conduct ourselves as professionals in our institutional lives. Another example is concealment of our spiritual, religious, or contemplative practice from the purview of our professional lives. Our group has been questioning the wisdom of such a stance and understanding. We believe in bringing the whole person and everything that the whole person entails—in short, the whole being—to bear upon our significant work and activities. It turns out, by Buddhist and other holistic understandings, that the whole human being implicates the entire cosmos.

Parker Palmer has inspired us with his declaration of "we teach who we are" (1998, p. 1). How are we to take this statement? I suggest that we need to take it as a general empirical statement: that's how it is and how it works. We cannot avoid bringing who we are into what we do and how we practice. Who we are just oozes out of ourselves and leaks into whatever we are doing, professionally or otherwise. But even if we somehow manage to do a reasonably good job of keeping the personal and professional separate and hermetically sealed, then this propensity and ability is also part of who we are, or, at least, who we appear to be, and permeates what we do and how we affect others. There is no escape. But beyond the facticity of non-separability of being and doing, the important question for us is, what do we do with this? So what if we teach who we are? What are the implications, and how do we work with it?

Avraham Cohen, who initiated this book project (and associated presentations at major conferences) with the five us—a team of university educators—declared a variation on Palmer's saying: "We teach who we are and that is the problem" (Cohen, 2009, p. 26). We may not intend to impact our students negatively, but if we as teachers have a certain negative manner of being, then this will negatively impact students. For example, if a person is highly anxious and tends to be defensive in her interaction with others, and this person conducts a class, chances are that her students will 'learn' to be anxious and ill at ease, and will end up with a lot of tension and stress, which will negatively impact not only their learning but also their personhood. I have witnessed this amongst some of my colleagues and their students. In fact, it does not matter if the teacher assures her students that they need not be anxious, and that they should relax, and so on. It is not the saying but the actual permeation of the group's conscious and unconscious by the teacher's being dimension (that is highly anxious in this case) that is the critical factor. Indeed, when there is a contradiction between the articulated message and 'signals' from the being dimension of the teacher, this creates a highly tense and likely psychologically difficult and even damaging situation that has been described as a double-bind. But not to dwell on the negative example only: if the teacher is an enthusiastic person full of excitement and passion for what he teaches and how he receives and interacts with his students, then this has a great and positive impact not only on what the students are learning but also who they are as persons and how they relate to the world. This speaks to the modeling dimension of teaching (Noddings, 1992), which is recognized for its supreme pedagogic importance.

Given the incredible power of 'we teach who we are,' how do we work with who we are and who our students are? First of all, we need to recognize that as educators, we are responsible for not only what we teach but also who we are and how we are. This recognition addresses the crucial importance of inner work; work that each of us undertakes with/in our selves in order to facilitate growth, authenticity, and wholeness as a person. But our recognition of the importance of inner work is not reflected in any teacher education we know of in North America. I am not aware of any teacher education program that pays attention to this. Maybe some reflective educators naturally and individually include inner work (whether it's called by that name or not) in their curriculum and pedagogy, but I have not known any teacher educator articulating it explicitly and working with it. In a culture that separates the personal from the professional, it would be hard to find teacher education programs that seriously incorporate inner work. Our inquiry and book project here is a response to this lack, and is based on our group's individual and collective work on who we are as educators. Each of us tells our tale of inner work. This chapter tells my tale, as a beginner, of inner work theory and practice.

INNER WORK

Here we are, seven billion of us, inhabiting a civilization that is increasingly proving to be environmentally and socially untenable and unsustainable. My colleagues and I have made the argument in various places (Bai, Donald & Scott, 2009; Bai & Scutt 2009; Bai, 2001) over the years that our education systems support this civilization by producing people who have internalized the values and beliefs of an untenable and unsustainable civilization best characterized as capitalistic consumerism backed up by militarism. I believe the only viable education that is open to us who are awakening to this understanding is one that helps and teaches us to deconstruct and reconstruct ourselves from inside out, from within the system, values and beliefs, and our habits of heart-mind—all that we have internalized. Let us call such inside-out de- and re-constructive work 'inner work' (Bai et al., forthcoming). It is an inner work in the sense that it is focused primarily on individuals changing the matrix of their own self-identity rather than primarily focusing on changing the external conditions and environments. To be clear, the inner work focus and the outer work focus should not be considered an exclusive duality. The relationship between the inner and the outer work is best represented by the imagery of möbius band. One flows and feeds into the other.

From my Buddhist and Daoist perspective on inner work, I see the inner work re-construction as primarily a removal of that which is not coherent with who we are as wholesome beings capable of lovingkindness, joy, compassion, and serenity. In the Buddhist tradition, such core humanity is known as bodhicitta—enlightened heart-mind—and is seen as our fundamental nature (Vokey, 2011). Inner work, if undertaken seriously, would change the world since what we do to the world and how we affect it has everything to do with the values and beliefs we carry about and enact, and attendant states of being or consciousness that permeate who we are. The old adage about the futility of putting old wine into a new wineskin makes sense. Revolutionaries of the world tend to focus on changing the wineskin, but without the change of fermenting old wine, we are soon back to the same state of sour smell in the new wineskin. Inner work does lead to outer transformation. Changing the world results from changing who you and I are in the being dimension. This kind of change has a deep educational implication. Our group of educators who teach teachers are interested in exploring and magnifying inner work in the field of education.

How do we then engage in inner work? Instead of explaining how this is done, I will share my own style of inner work. For the remainder of this writing, I engage in a series of what I call 'Reminders' in which I engage in re-mind-ing, that is, re-conditioning my heart-mind.

Reminder One: Look for the Original Face

Last night at a public panel presentation that featured an impressive cadre of educators, academicians, and spiritual teachers, a debate broke out over human nature. The drift of the debate went like this: In the face of so much violence, suffering, deceit, greed, and environmental degradation worldwide, it is difficult to defend a positive view of human nature—that it is fundamentally or primordially compassionate, wise, generous, and loving. At one point of this dark debate, however, one woman rose up and shared her story of looking into a newborn baby's eyes and seeing utter openness and vulnerability, and how that moment profoundly changed her view of humanity. It was such a singular and transformative experience for her that it changed her life and career. She came to affirm the possibility that humans were capable of becoming wise, compassionate, and loving-caring. Hearing the story, I was deeply moved, for I was reminded of my own singular experience, and because of this, I could resonate deeply with what I heard. I too looked into such eyes and met, in astonishment, a completely open gaze: those of my own daughters shortly after they were born. It is experience like this that suggests to us that the lack of compassion, generosity, and love and care in human beings signals that something utterly unfortunate happened to compromise, diminish, or even destroy humanity.

Here is an analogy I would like to present. Newborn children, unless perhaps there is some genetic or structural damage, are capable of learning any of a few hundred human languages. Learning, however, is a process of converting capacity to ability. We may be capable of speaking hundreds of different languages, but in most cases, we end up with one spoken language, unless attempts are made to exercise the capacity. Likewise, we are capable of embodying the deepest and widest possibilities of humanity, such as penetrating wisdom, boundless love and compassion at a cosmic scale, and unsuppressible joy of being. I would like to remind readers that such humanity is our birthright.

Yet just how much of such possibility becomes actualized is mostly a matter of learning. We become what we are taught to be. We can learn to become insecure, fearful, anxious, selfish, mean-spirited, greedy, violent, and cruel; or the opposite; or somewhere in-between for most of us. The 'lessons' in this learning come to us by way of how our parents and others close to us treat us with all those countless looks, gestures, talks, whispers, and all manners of interaction, instruction, and injunction, said and unsaid, including how they interpret the world for us, show us in action, and the same is reinforced in school, media, and other public institutions. These lessons are, like the air we breathe, invisible in the sense 'we see them but we don't really see them.' The problem with the human nature debate is the confusion: what we are debating about is not really human nature but human learning. The dark and tragic view of the so-called human nature—that we are selfish, insecure, and even cruel—is more about the dark and tragic view and practice by which we learn, mostly unconsciously, to be such people, and less about who we are in our capacity for humanity. And it might be instructive for us to inquire where this dark view originates and how it is reinforced, and why it is so strong in our culture and civilization. One source—but not the only source—may lie in the Judeo-Christian traditions that have a basis in the metaphor of original sin. This view is deeply entrenched in western civilization. (I am relieved to know that not all Christians believe in Original Sin, and some even believe in Original Blessings!)

It is instructive to remind ourselves that this grim view is not shared by all cultures and traditions. In one tradition that I am familiar with, namely Zen Buddhism, our natural capacity is known as 'the original face before our parents were born,' or more simply, 'the original face before I was born.' It alludes to reality of human nature that precedes and goes beyond one's particular socio-cultural and psychological construction. As such, the original face reflects unconditioned inner radiance and compassion. Recovering, getting in touch with, and rebirthing this original face are the spiritual work from the Buddhist perspective. The Daoist tradition also has a positive view of human nature/capacity. Using the archetypal metaphors of 'baby' and the feminine,

EDUCATION FOR ENLIGHTENMENT

Daoism also points to our vast and inherent capacity for openness, receptivity, and creativity. To repeat, this is our natural birthright. Yet, we so easily lose sight of it.

THE ORIGINAL FACE BEFORE I WAS BORN

I am seated in my cross-legged meditation position. Another radiant day with bright sun and blue sky in Vancouver. Yet my inner sun is dim, and the inner horizons are not vast and brilliantly blue. I feel dull and dispirited. It's time for our morning meditation. Avraham, my partner, strikes the brass bowl three times, each peal penetrating deeper into my consciousness. I am searching for my original face before I was born—my Zen face. How deeply buried it seems to be this morning! Beneath my grimace of anxiety, resentment, worry . . . many thick layers to peel off to allow my original face to shine through. My life memories recent and distant flood in. I am re-living these experiences from my past in the moment. Worries and fear grip me when I think of my precious daughters' and their possible progenies on this rapidly degenerating planet. But how my precious children differ from the street people I run into on my street who too were once newborns! I am aware that I have suddenly widened my focus from my personal family to the family of all beings. This increases my despair and fear. My fear is now changing to hatred and aggression. My mind goes to the familiar place of finding some people or some institutions to blame. Ignorant politicians! Another shift: Anger and resentment seize me as thoughts of a colleague whose ways of relating and treating students caused so much grief and trouble recently. I find my mind getting more and more mired in the negative details and agitating. I feel increasing heaviness and suffocating sense in my chest. Emotionally I feel like I am imploding or exploding. Life becomes unbearable. Affliction! The First Noble Truth that the historical Buddha taught! Here we go! Okay, it's hopeless to control the thickly rising thoughts that cloud my consciousness. I know it's not a matter of will and control. I know what I need to do: I take refuge in each breath. One deep breath. Another deep breath. One more. One more. Long and slow, with each exhalation through my pursed lips. Gradually—how long have I been sitting?—my awareness shifts and lifts. As I take in each life-giving breath, worries depart and fear calms down, even though somewhat reluctantly; anger softens by degrees, and anxiety lifts like a coastal fog. I feel immensely relieved. Gratitude floods in. So does an inner light. It feels as though a warm glowing lamp got turned on from within. At last, I have come to the face that beams in radiance and smiles in bliss. Is this the Original Face? Hello! At the same time, I still feel a lingering measure of anxiety—of losing this peaceful but probably very short-lived moment of grace. Clinging onto the experience of bliss is futile, and precipitates another round of torment. Let go of even bliss. Palms up and hands extended in a gesture of letting go. It is easy to forget that, in the midst of all our daily trials and afflictions, the original face of humanity is still there, ready to shine through even if only momentarily. What is important is that I get in touch with it every day.

Reminder Two: Affirm the primacy of being over having/doing

I am a product of Korean education that was (and still is) driven by Examination Hell. I am also a product of a family that survived the brutality of Japanese colonization and the Korean War, both of which took place against the backdrop of worldwide westernization and modernization. As the youngest born arriving after the war, I escaped the direct assault of both the colonization and the war that my family suffered first-hand. But just as second-hand smoke is almost equally damaging, so is the second-hand trauma of growing up in a family (and in a nation) that suffered from an immense amount of brutality, deprivation, and survival stress. The determination to survive and succeed was total and uncompromising in my family. I grew up receiving the message, implicit and explicit, from my family and from the culture, that schooling is the only means to ensure my social and economic survival and leading a decent life. This was not a deceptive message: the Korean social reality confirmed it. Thus I spent my initial and formative 12 years going through the examination hell driven Korean schooling. I knew no life other than studying slavishly hard every day from morning till night, perpetually coping with fear and anxiety associated with doing well in school. The fear of not doing well in tests and examinations, and ending up with poor grades, which would take away my chance to enter a high-ranking university, was my constant companion. All social security and mobility in Korea are tied up tightly with the rank-ordered schooling system. Even for girls whose only career in life tended to be mothering, it is important to go to a high-ranking university because that is where they will meet their future husbands who will work for high-ranking corporations.

I am still hearing from my Korean friends, some of whom are veteran schoolteachers and school counsellors in Korea, that the pressure on school children, now as young as four and five in kindergartens, is far worse than what we experienced many decades ago. I get the same message from my current Chinese students who are doing their graduate degrees in my university: young children stay up till 11 o'clock every night studying. My Japanese colleagues tell me that essentially the same story holds in Japan as well. Are we doing better in North America? If comparison to Asian countries is what we are after, I would say: Yes. North American students are not quite so chained and pressured. But the idea of putting children through a system of schooling in which they are compelled to learn something or another, compelled to work (study) and produce (test results), and that their self-worth is predominantly tied to school performance and productivity is the same everywhere. Differences between east and west are only a matter of degree. The oppressive patterns are not different here. These practices are normalized and entrenched, and we do nothing more than complain about how our curriculum is out-dated or does not yield the result we want, namely making our children more competent and smart, and more prepared to win the competition for the best job, the best house, the best partner, and so on. What we do not ask is what this kind of education is doing to the well-being and humanity of our children, and by extension, to ourselves. What kind of people are we creating, and by extension, what kind of civilization on this planet? I suggest that what we are doing to our children in the name of education is violation of their natural birthright—the right to peace, joy, love, and happiness in the company of all beings on this planet. How can I be making such a case when we, parents and teachers, are so dedicated to our children's learning, and pour so much resources into education, and try really hard to make learning 'fun' and useful? And we educators and parents work really very hard! But slave traders work hard too. So do prison guards.

There is no question about all of us—parents, educators, students, and administrators—all working very hard. Also, there is no question that most of us are well meaning and want to see our children and students succeed and have a good life. However, these are not the issues. The question we need to ask is, what about the sanity and well-being of our children and ourselves?

PLEASE LEAD ME TO THE FIELD OF BEING

Now that my mom is physically no more on this planet, she seems to have taken up a virtual residence within my psyche. Here and there, now and then, often out of nowhere and suddenly, I feel her vivid presence. I have also gotten into the habit of addressing her.

Um-ma ('Mom' in Korean), I know you believed that you had no choice but to keep pushing me to study hard and succeed in school. That's how the Korean social system worked, and still does. You were so proud of me because I was a winner as a student. You were so pleased when I graduated with a doctorate. I fulfilled your dream—the dream of achieving social and material success through schooling, which you yourself could not realize because of your poor peasant background. You worshipped education because you saw, correctly in our case, that it was the only road to social success open to people without the prior advantage of wealth and class. You were right. Now your children, with three PhDs, one MD, and one wealthy businesswoman, are leading materially comfortable and professionally respected lives. You succeeded beyond measure! But there is an insidious cost to such success. Do you know that? Do you know that it's difficult for me to relax and do nothing, to enjoy just being? Growing up in Korea, and having been raised by you, known to be the Tiger Woman in your younger days, striving and achieving were inscribed into my very nervous system. But, as a teacher, how can I be a model of a balanced and wholesome human being for my students? I've got to live the values I teach: the primacy of being over having and doing and the primacy of intrinsic valuing over instrumentalism. So, Um-ma, now please help me to learn and grow in the dimension of being. Just as you held my little hand and walked me to school, now lead me to the Field of Being that you must be more familiar with in this next life of yours.

Reminder Three: Awaken and Nurture the Soul

Notwithstanding all the well-meaning people and their hard work, and notwithstanding all the care, generosity, and love being practiced every where, much of the world today in industrial civilization is caught up in conditions of alienation and discontent, and locked into a cycle of insatiable consumerism and ever-grinding production. Commodification has come to define every aspect of life on this planet. The wheel of existence that the Hindus and the Buddhists talk about has turned into the capitalist wheel of production and consumption. At present our civilization seems to have one purpose only: to keep this wheel moving and rolling—relentlessly. There shall be no stop or slow down in the production of consumable goods and services, and to support that, consumption must be kept up. The advertising industry uses most advanced psychologists to study how human desire works and how it can be maximally stimulated for the purpose of thirsting after consumable goods and services. Basically humanity is chained to this psychological machinery of ever-thirsting and never-fulfilled desire, which is then further chain-linked to the work world of service and production. We must ask, then, what kind of people does our systems of education have to generate to sustain this juggernaut? The answer: People who are driven to work all the time, who value themselves and others primarily on the basis of what they earn, gain, achieve, win, produce, and consume. They must not experience, neither readily nor deeply, contentment, vitality, inner peace and joy, and love of what is here and now. In fact, they must constantly feel the gnawing dissatisfaction, unrest, and inadequacy, and a sense of gaping insecurity, anxiety, and emptiness: in short, what Buddhists call '*dukkha*'. They must habitually think in terms of 'only if' and 'only when,' and convert all their current misery and dissatisfaction into dreams of future fulfillment through owning and consuming more and better. They must feel greedy, competitive, and insecure about their entitlement. Fear and anxiety, and inadequacy and insufficiency, greed, envy and resentment, must be their constant companions like their own long shadows. Indeed, these are their psychological shadows. They must always put themselves on the constant verge of time-stress and deadline distress, and worry that they are losing and wasting time, and are not getting enough done. They should see the universe as an indifferent place—the Cartesian 'mere extension'—and life as fundamentally meaningless, and feel no kinship or inter-being (Nhat Hahn, 1998) with the earth community, for it is out of such meaninglessness and disconnect that the soul dreams a nightmare of consumerism as its fulfillment.

The hemlock for this culture is well distributed throughout educational system and practices. I dare say that our schooling is set up, by and large, to disengage and numb the consciousness of our children with a staggering amount of discursive and abstract information that is pumped into them with the expectation that they will pump it back out. We (generally speaking) overwhelm them with time-pressure that precipitates stress-induced diseases in varying degrees and in various ways. We continuously distract them with externally driven demands and rewards so that they are prevented from being in touch with what is happening within them and around them. They become distanced from their own reality of mind-body-heart-spirit. 'Good' students are those who do not keel over from the stress, learn the routine of information overload and discharging, learn to re-orient themselves from the internally-informed to externally-informed mode of action, and who learn to accept the substitution of reality by various simulacra. And part of this learning to accept substitution is forgetting the blissful experience of being alive, being here-and-now, and replacing it by short-lived and never-fulfilled, therefore, continually pursued desires for pleasures and satisfaction that involve having objects, services, and substances. Recall Socrates' reminder to his fellow Athenians 2,500 years ago: that they were paying attention to wealth, fame, and status, but neglecting to care about improving or perfecting their soul (as cited in Tredennick, 1954). I think the most lucid way to understand the function of 'soul' is that it is the existential core of our selves, like *bodhicitta* (*awakened heart-mind*), that directly and sensitively touches reality, and is capable of joy and happiness, wisdom and compassion, and is full of vitality and creativity. If this capacity to experience bliss is so core to our selves, then the fact that for most of us this capacity has shrivelled or that it has been displaced massively by materialistic consumption, should tell us that there has been some major damage to this capacity.

Good students are those who will become 'good' citizens, fit into the triple-formation of industry-military-entertainment complex, and perform endless routine tasks around the clock, whether in offices or in factories, and accept the substitution gratification of small pleasures like exotic vacations and new consumer merchandise. This regimen of substitution gratification starts early: teachers putting stars on our homework, receiving good grades, awards, and privileged treatment, and the emotional and material reward system that our parents mount. By the time we reach young adulthood, we are heavily inducted into the worldview of careerism, consumerism, and workaholism. Senseless? A permanent state of distress from time pressure and other externally imposed demands becomes a sign of normalcy and maturity.

Most parents and teachers mean well, and want their children and students to 'succeed' in the world. Herein lies the problem. To succeed in the present civilization, people need to be anxious, insecure, greedy, insatiable, and working and pushing themselves all the time. 'Teaching' people to be this way is the hidden curriculum of our school today. Every aspect of school life, including curriculum and pedagogy, is creating, even if unwittingly, people who are slaves to the soul-destroying juggernaut. School children learn early that they need to earn good grades to be respected and approved by their teachers, peers, and even by their parents. They are coaxed, lured, and compelled to learn stuff for which they have no intrinsic desire or motivation. Before long, their intrinsic agency, such as curiosity, love, and enjoyment, is replaced by external control such as fear of losing or desire for gaining. Soon they speak the language of compulsion and compliance: 'I had to do . . .' 'they made me do . . .' As well, they speak the language of instrumentalism: doing something for reasons of money, job, status, approval, and so on. They have lost their soul. Anytime we stress ourselves relentlessly and accumulatively, and live routinely in the zone of 'fight, flight, or freeze' responses, sooner than later, we become 'drained' and 'burnt out.' We become soulless.

BOOTSTRAPPING MY SOUL

It is one thing to discourse about the lamentable state of soul loss in the world, and another to do something about it in one's own being. The task is particularly onerous, for it is a catch-22 situation. One needs a soul to deal with one's soul loss! True. But as long as there is enough soul left to initiate the regeneration, all is not lost. From this hopeful place within me, I ask myself: where do I begin this regeneration of my soul? Who in me answers my question? I ask and then wait . . . for a part of me to show up and answer. I wait. Now I hear: begin where the soul manifests, however fleetingly and seemingly small ways. This is intriguing. It's as though there are more than one part to me. That's good. We need a dialogue! Listen, more's coming . . . The moment my heart delights and my face lights up, at that moment my soul is shining through. Joy, gladness, gratitude, and wonder: these are the signs of my soul's presence. I am learning to notice, recognize, and acknowledge these moments of presence. Indeed, every moment contains such presence. My meditation practice is one way for me to learn to notice these moments and to identify and deconstruct those structures in my consciousness that are in the way of this 'shining through.' According to the eminent Buddhist scholar and teacher, Robert Thurman, "Reality itself is bliss!" (Thurman, 2008, April. Buddhism as a civilization matrix and the current global crisis. Public talk, University of British Columbia, Vancouver, Canada) In other words, the possibilities of experiencing joy are infinite. Given such possibilities, how is that that I am—many of us are—so prone to dis-ease and dis-content, in one degree or another, in one form or another? Back to my answer: loss of soul. I am reflecting all the ways throughout my growing-up years at home and at school in which my joy receptor—soul—was dampened, harassed, and badly addled. No one set out to destroy my soul. Of course not. On the contrary, everyone around me was deeply interested and invested in my receiving a good education and becoming successful. But therein lies the problem: my attention and energy—the soul's material—was continually siphoned out of me in the name of education. I could not attend to, and give birth to, each moment's pregnant possibility of joy and wonder because I was required to be mostly elsewhere, not where I wanted and needed to be: beside me, inside me, with me, uninterrupted, unobstructed—fully present. What does being fully present feel like? A sudden flashback from my childhood—I am six or seven—I am little Heesoon and I am crouching down for a long spell of time in the backyard of my house by a fist-sized puddle hole created by the rain dripping down from the roof's gutter. All the dirt is washed away, and only pebbles remain in the water-filled hole. It is a miniature tidal pool. I do not know how many countless hours I've spent gazing into the pool, sometime introducing new pebbles and beads I found, and raptly watching the ring of ripples when rain drops fall. It is totally magical to me, and I am in another world—in my own matrix, another state of consciousness—in bliss. I now know the name of such state: contemplative consciousness. Such consciousness occurs, as in my example from childhood, naturally and spontaneously. Sooner or later, most children get trained out of it more or less. Finding my way back into it is my idea of bootstrapping the soul.

Reminder Four: Play not Panic

In states of extreme stress, people go into panic. They lose all sense of perspective and bearing, and start to run around senselessly. My observations of the world we live in today convince me that collectively our civilization has reached a state of panic. We have lost the internal guidance system that would tell us when to slow down, rest, sleep, play, contemplate, and recharge. Without such internal guidance, we run ourselves down until we collapse. An animal seized by panic will run around directionless, in fact, often right into the open jaws of a predator. It has lost its ability to see what's going on in the environment. It literally loses sight of what is right before it. It is experiencing tunnel vision. Here is a case narrative I read (Fehmi & Robbins, 2007): a child who lived in terror of his father's violent abuse and neglect was brought to a specialist. The child was lagging far behind in reading competency and suffering from severe anxiety. The specialist found out, through tests and talking to the child, that when he reads, his field of vision narrows to the point that he can only see one letter at a time! Fortunately, the attention specialist who figured out what was going on with this child (a child suffering from 'reading trauma'!) was able to 'teach' the child to bring about sufficient relaxation in himself that his vision widened to include words, and make sense of them in the context of sentences and paragraphs. This is a remarkable story, indeed, and a teaching story for me. There is a whole civilizational implication here. A society hooked on speed and short-term solutions to everything, and unable to look beyond the usual three-year planning (compared to, say, seven generations) for consequences of our action, looks to me like one driven by panic and terror. We are not able to 'read' the book of life. Our reading comprehension of the world is extremely constricted. Evidence of this lies in the way we go on abusing the planet and assaulting human communities. The business-as-usual mannerism is not anything 'cool', but panicking animals' stunned response to circumstances that are incomprehensible and deeply threatening. How do we bring about sufficient relaxation to our whole being so that we can see beyond our nose, and all the immediate busy tasks that consume so much of our waking hours? This is a civilizational question in that the survival and sustainability of the whole civilization (and its responsibility to the biosphere as a whole) crucially depends on the shift in our consciousness from panic to mindfulness or reflective awareness.

When our vision is tightly constricted, we lose the breadth in our field of vision. We see only one thing and lose all sight of the background. We are not in the field. We only see objects in front of our nose, and at worst, not even the whole object.

When our being is so constricted, we lose the field of play, and we don't know the space in which we can make our movements and moves. We cannot play. Not even the game of chase and chased. We freeze.

Learning and panic are antithetical. No learning can happen when learners are unable to stay in a Field of Being and make creative moves, even including unlearning. For new learning to take place, unlearning old patterns (habits) of perception, interpretation, and how-to's are necessary. A panic-driven animal is unable to be creative. It only repeats what it knows, movement after movement, even if these are fancy and complex movements. It may move, but has no clear sense of directions based on the perception of reality and what is happening in its environment. For sure, the more stressful I perceive and experience a circumstance to be, the more likely I am to lose my consciousness and freedom of choice, and the more likely I am to fall back into stereotyped, deeply inscribed, archaic patterns of reaction. Civilizationally we seem to be permanently gripped in a state of panic. It is not that there is no guidance about the directions we need to take. What is disordering the planet and ailing the hearts and minds of people has been said and heard over and over again. But this knowledge is not being acted upon in any coherent and ordered way. When a person is in a state of panic, telling and shouting to them which direction to turn and run falls on a deaf ear. He cannot make sense of what he hears. So he runs around until no more running can happen: exhaustion and/or death are the outcomes. It's probably fair to say that we have become numbed to these warnings by over-exposure to repetitious and increasingly shrill warnings of doom. Panic has become a way of life. Is there a sense that we are educating people to be in a chronic and unrecognized state of panic? Perhaps it is fair to say that we have all been pushed and stretched so far that we don't even feel the panic anymore. Getting back in touch with this feeling would be a move, albeit an unpleasant one, in the right direction.

It seems the academy is prone to this dis-ease. A colleague in my university once told me that she saw the world in colour again once she received tenure! This story in its own way is as drastic and distressing as the story of the little boy who was unable to read and make sense of what he reads. The ill-logic is the same. Anytime we stress ourselves relentlessly and accumulatively, we become fish without water, birds without air, wizards drained of wizardry.

LEARNING TO PLAY

> *I sit facing my therapist. She hands me a basket of colourful hand-dyed yarn balls. She suggests to me that I can put the strings around my chair in any way and manner I feel like. She called it putting the boundary around me. At first I misunderstand her meaning. I don't want boundaries—they would feel imprisoning to me! After some hands-on experience with the exercise, and getting feedback from my therapist on what my experiences are with this exercise, I come to the understanding that the boundary is really about demarcating the space within which I would feel safe and secure to play. It is like setting up a playpen for myself. I am marking out my space of play—space in which I can express my creativity and be playful.*

I began my work with this therapist trained in body-oriented psychotherapy to address my tension and stress problems. When I experience tension and stress, there is this sense of reality pressing right into my face, and there is literally little room to move or breathe. Mentally I thrash around when that happens. I feel trapped. A sense of panic hits me, and the first thing I notice is how my peripheral vision has diminished. So does the ability to see distance. Perspective disappears. A sense of flatness comes over me. And I am not amusing to anyone, including myself. Humour has departed. Humourless, witless, smile-less. In short, I am no more homo ludens (human the player); I am homo panikos (human the panic-stricken). I am really sad.

What was the origin and history of my becoming a homo panikos? I cannot date it to the first instance, but I am familiar with the tension and stress that I endured throughout my schooling years and probably earlier. Endless and countless tests and exams: accumulation of deep psychological stress. On the days that I was not too well prepared to write my exams, I would suffer from particular tension and stress, and I kept thinking that hell must be just like this. (Now I know that humans do worse things to themselves and to each other.) We make our children go through experiences like this all in the name of 'for your own good.' There is always some moral justification for torture. Little tortures lead to unimaginably ugly tortures. I don't think I can ever be a schoolteacher for young children. No amount of 'it's for your own good' can convince my mind or my body to carry out any educational measures that will inflict stress, pain, and harm, and drive children to a state of panic, however minor. How can we justify an education that induces panic? The only justifiable education is one that teaches students to create a greater and greater space of play where they can do the interpretive dance with and for life. The greater the space of play, the greater the scope and intensity of creativity.

I have become a teacher of teachers. Leading education out of panic and into play will be my life mission. But for me to do this, I must be simultaneously working on healing my own panic-driven soul, and this will allow transformation of my panic into play. Do I hear the sound of a flute? May I dance?

> *Dance when you're broken open.*
> *Dance when you've torn the bandage off.*
> *Dance in the middle of fighting.*
> *Dance in your blood.*
> *Dance when you're perfectly free.*
> *Struck, the dancer hears a tambourine inside her,*
> *like a wave that crests into foam at the very top,*
> *Begins.*

Maybe you don't hear that tambourine,
or the tree leaves clapping time.
Close the ears on your head,
that listen mostly to lies and cynical jokes.
There are other things to see, and hear.
Music. Dance.
A brilliant city inside your soul!
(Rumi, as cited in Barks, 2004, p. 281)

REFERENCES

Bai, H., Cohen, A., Culham, T., Park, S., Rabi, S., Scott, C., & Tait, S. (forthcoming). Moving Through the Dao-field of Life, Aware, Balanced, Aligned, and Connected. In Gunnlaugson, O., Sarath, E., Scott, C. & Bai, H. (Eds.), *Contemplative approaches to learning and inquiry across disciplines.* New York: SUNY Press.

Bai, H., Donald, B. & Scott, C. (2009). Contemplative pedagogy and revitalization of teacher education. *Alberta Journal of Educational Research, 55*(3), 319–334.

Bai, H. & Scutt, G. (2009). Touching the earth with the heart of enlightened mind: A Buddhist contribution to ecology as educational practice. *Canadian Journal of Environmental Education, 14*, 92–106.

Bai, H. (2001). Challenge for education: Learning to value the world intrinsically. *Encounter, 14*(1), 4–16.

Barks, C., Rumi, J. & J. Moyne, J. (2004). *The essential Rumi* (A. Arberry, C. Barks, J. Moyne, & R. Nicholson, Transl.). New York: HarperCollins.

Cohen, A. (2009). *Gateway to the Dao-field: Essays for the awakening educator.* Amherst, NY: Cambria.

Fehmi, L. & Robbins, J. (2007), *The open-focus brain.* London: Trumpeter Books.

Noddings, N. (1992). *The challenge to care in schools.* New York: Teachers College Press, Columbia University.

Nhat Hahn, T. (1998). *Interbeing* (3rd ed.). Berkeley, CA: Parallax Press.

Palmer, P. (1998). *The courage to teach.* San Francisco: Jossey-Bass.

Tredennick, H. (1954). *Plato: The last days of Socrates.* Middlesex, England: Penguin Books.

Vokey, D. (2011). Moral education for the 21st century: A Buddhist view. In J. DeVitis and T. Yu (Eds.), *Character and moral education: A reader.* New York: Peter Lang .

INNERWORKINGS

CARL LEGGO

POETIC INQUIRY

*M*ost *of my life I have been a religious seeker* . . .

POETIC INQUIRY

Most of my life I have been a religious seeker. On Career Day in high school, I was the only student who attended the session with a local Christian minister. And, through all the twists and turns in my life, I have spent most Sunday mornings in buildings with communities of other religious seekers calling out to God in the name of Jesus. I might not like much of Christendom (including fearful faith, legalistic literalism, poisoned piety, and self-serving sanctimony), but I like Christ—a lot (especially his pedagogical heart, prophetic voice, poetic imagination, and provocative courage). Franck (1993) called himself part of 'The New Order,' which he described as "the anonymous, unorganized, organic network of awareness beyond all ideological labels, born under the lash of anxiety on the threshold of our collective suicide" (p. 23). I too recognize my connection to Franck's 'New Order:'

> It is a network of loners, encompassing those who reflect on the meaning of being Human in our technotronic rat trap, who dare to fathom the depths of life, of death, in order to attain a life-praxis, an ethos suitable for this end-time: a religious orientation to existence. Without badge, without watchword, they recognize, hearten one another. (Franck, 1993, pp. 23–24)

Taking up Franck's notion of 'a religious orientation to existence,' I am called to read again the stories that have mapped my understanding of 'inner life.' I have always longed for a religious orientation to existence, but I have never been very happy with most of what I have known to comprise religious experience. The word religion has intriguing etymological possibilities. While the word is frequently defined by 'to tie, fasten, or bind,' as in establishing an obligation between humans and gods, there is also a connection to literacy, as in 'to read again, to go through again.' In order to understand the complex and convoluted and conflicted stories that shape my experience of 'inner life,' I need to learn how 'to read again, to go through again' my autobiographical texts as a religious seeker.

Atwood (2002) reminded us that "what we consider real is also imagined: every life lived is also an inner life, a life created" (p. 7). So, what is real and what is imagined? What is inner life and what is outer life? Have I been too religiously bound to a binary opposition that valorizes one kind of experience over another? Have I been guilty of fragmentation and compartmentalization?

Palmer (2004) promoted a thoughtful understanding of living experience: "Afraid that our inner light will be extinguished or our inner darkness exposed, we hide our true identities from each other. In the process, we become separated from our own souls" (p. 4). When I first read Palmer's claims about 'inner light' and 'inner darkness,' I began questioning his readiness to reiterate the traditional binary opposition between light and dark. I asked: What is this 'undivided life' that Palmer is so keen to see transformed into wholeness? What if we begin with a notion that everything is whole to begin with? Even more taxing, I think, is

Palmer's reference to 'our own souls.' What is this soul? Is it an essence? A spirit? A divine spark? An embodied fire? I like the word, just like I like soul music with its plaintive rhythms that remind me of the heart's slow breathing. But do I really know my soul any more than I know soul music? Would I recognize my soul if I met it on a Saturday afternoon at the shopping mall?

Regarding Palmer's notion of a hidden wholeness, perhaps I want the holes more than the wholeness. Steeped in post-modernism, I am plural, multiple, in process, ecologically and ethically and aesthetically and etymologically evolving. According to Palmer, "the divided life may be endemic, but wholeness is always a choice. Once I have seen my dividedness, do I continue to live a contradiction—or do I try to bring my inner and outer worlds back into harmony?" (p. 17) As I continued to read Palmer, I grew more and more concerned with his Quaker enthusiasm for 'inner and outer worlds' like an adolescent discussion of the aesthetics of innie and outie bellybuttons. But regardless of any concerns I might experience while reading Palmer, he is always a lot more fun than most authors, so I continued to read, to read again, to tie my text to Palmer's text, and then I found his use of the concept of the Möbius strip, which is an intriguing geometric shape, a loop that looks like it has two surfaces, while it actually has a continuous one-sided surface. Palmer was not promoting binary oppositions at all. As Palmer noted, "there is no 'inside' and 'outside' on the Möbius strip" (p. 47). Palmer wisely claimed that while our culture "separates inner from outer, private from public, personal from professional" (p. 47), "we all live on the Möbius strip all the time: there is no place to hide!" (p. 47) The Möbius strip invites an understanding of turning and returning, of reading again, of living the familiar with new possibilities for the unfamiliar. Life is not linear, not only birth and death with some chronology in between, filled with frequent errors and occasional successes. Life is breath, spirit, movement, dance, creation, and imagination.

Like any preacher, pedagogue, prophet, Palmer's words are more evocative invitations to conversation than rock-hard slabs of truth. When Palmer writes, "we can be peacemakers in our small part of the world only when we are at peace within ourselves" (p. 174), I admire the tender thought, but I also know it hangs by a slender thread. If I can only be a peacemaker when I am at peace within myself, then I will never make peace. I am far too piecemeal for peace. I am competitive, lustful, self-righteous. I always want more than I need. I want to win the lottery even if I don't purchase tickets. I want to make more money. I want want want with whining wanton wishy-washiness. So, how can I ever be at peace? Peace will remain pea-sized in my soul, a speck of yeast, still perhaps, a fleck of leaven, at least, that might possibly lead to living and loving, to living love.

Conjunctions

while I once sought the whole
I only ever found holes

because I can never tell

a whole story, I seek fragments

since I am an incomplete sentence
I seek communion with others

like the possibilities of conjunctions
ghosts are everywhere, everywhen

as they call us eagerly to connect
like bridges that lean on light

with invitations to walk in places
where we have been but never been

conjunctions invite us to know interconnections, even if our eyes are dim

REFERENCES

Atwood, M. (2002). *Negotiating with the dead: A writer on writing.* Cambridge: Cambridge University Press.
Franck, F. (1993). *A little compendium on that which matters.* New York: St. Martin's.
Palmer, P. J. (2004). *A hidden wholeness: The journey toward an undivided life.* San Francisco: Jossey-Bass.

LIVING POETICALLY

A Teacher's Credo

I have lived my life with love.
(Freire, 1993, p. 88)

Applicants for wisdom
do what I have done:
inquire within.
(Heraclitus, 2001, p. 51)

Love and revolution go together.
(Freire, 1993, p. 87)

Just as the river where I step
is not the same, and is,
so I am as I am not.
(Heraclitus, 2001, p. 51)

I Am

I am a boy
whose tongue
is stained
with wild blueberries.

I am a man
whose past
lingers like
a long evening tattoo.

I am from the east and the west.

I Am, said God.
Nothing more.
No predicate.
Revealed, concealed,
never congealed.
Like Madonna or Cher,
one simple name,

an iconic sign
with folds of identity.

Unlike my I am, followed
by an abecedarian
of modifiers all seeking
to spell my mystery.

But still

I am
not sure who
I am.

Even after exhausting
all the possibilities of I am,
I could still spill I am not
in an endless list,
an infinite deferral,
a fierce scribbling
of lines with no X.

I am. Am I?

Canadian historian Akenson (1998) wrote that "tough, wonderful texts are, at heart, all the same and . . . one approaches them with reverence" (p. xi). Akenson is writing specifically about the Bible and the Talmud, texts that have compelled generations of readers, but I suggest that Akenson reminded us to consider our role in response to all texts, including the texts of our own vocation or calling as educators. I have been a student or a teacher all my life. While I have held a few summer jobs as a lifeguard, stevedore, block-handler, and newspaper delivery person, I have been in school since I was four years old. I am now 57. For more than a half century I have been connected with schools of some kind—12 years as a student in elementary and secondary schools, nine years as a teacher in secondary schools, 12 years as a student in universities, here and there, and 21 years as a professor at the University of British Columbia. That is my life story. It doesn't take long to live more than half a century. But it takes a long time to make sense of the stories lived so quickly that it is hard to remember where one has been, hard to imagine where one might go.

Akenson wrote that "tough, wonderful texts are, at heart, all the same and . . . one approaches them with reverence" (p. xi). The autobiographical story of my education is a tough text full of wonder, and, if I ever hope to make sense of it, I need to approach it with reverence. Woodruff (2001) proposed "that we restore the idea of reverence to its proper place in ethical and political thought" (p. 38). And I want to add educational thought as well. "To teach reverence," suggested Woodruff, "you must find the seeds of reverence in each person and help them grow" (p. 13). That is, and has always been, my starting place.

The word credo means I believe, but it also more accurately signifies: I have given my heart to.

So, as an educator, I ask, what have I given my heart to?

The way up is the way back. (Heraclitus, 2001, p. 45)

In my first year of teaching, 1976, at R. W. Parsons Collegiate in Robert's Arm, Newfoundland, I taught a grade seven class with 48 students. (One of those students is now the city manager in Lethbridge, Alberta, but that's another story.) I was 22-years old, I had a lot of clothes from Tip Top, and a couple degrees from Memorial University. I was writing a master's thesis on the novels of Rosamond Lehmann. I had been married for two years, and I owned a new Chevrolet truck. I had been exploring Christianity for a year, and I was beginning to think that I might like to be a United Church minister.

Forty-eight grade seven students are a lot of students, and many of them didn't really want to be in school. Many of them didn't know what they were doing in school. The few who wanted to be in school were often upset with everybody else for being noisy nuisances. I worked hard on classroom management or control or discipline. Like the carnival game where you smack gophers that randomly pop up out of holes, I grew more violent as September seeped through my skin. Near the end of September, Sylvia who was 13 and looked 16 and acted like she was six going on 36, did something or said something or looked something (I can't remember since every day brought new catastrophes and crises and conundrums enough to overstuff my memory, and Sylvia was often the grinning face at the centre of most challenges) that ignited a moment full of momentous teaching and learning.

I remember I was standing at the side of my teacher's desk (one of those big boxy hardwood desks that provides a sense of security when you huddled behind it). I guess I was teaching—talking at least, almost certainly pontificating in my emerging teacher's voice, just as new and officious as my Tip Top tweed sport jacket. I don't remember anything really, but I assume that Sylvia or one of the other 48 students said or did something that triggered an explosion inside me. All I remember is that I was standing beside my teacher's desk, and then I was standing on my teacher's desk, knees slightly bent and arms curled, like the Incredible Hulk when he bursts into a green rage. I looked at my students. They looked fearful. No one spoke or moved. The moment was an etched tableau. I didn't know how I had jumped from the floor to the desk. I still don't think it's physically possible to jump that high from a still position. All I know is I had lost my mind and gained superhuman strength. I looked at my students, and I knew there was only one response left. I laughed. Then they giggled. At first softly, then a little louder. Our laughter gurgled like water flowing in a blocked pipe that has just been augured. I jumped off the desk and we all laughed a long time. I'm not sure what any of us learned in that moment, but whatever I learned has lingered with me a long long time.

CARL LEGGO

Night's Patience

Forgotten words
rise like turnips
in a moon-tugged field.

Each morning I wake
with a trace of soil
around my lips.

Perhaps in the long
night when I assume
I am lost in sleep

I am really pulling
carrots with my teeth,
calling forgotten words,

knowing always how
nothing is ever lost,
only buried, waiting.

      So, as an educator, I ask, what have I given my heart to?

> Whoever cannot seek
> the unforeseen sees nothing,
> for the known way
> is an impasse.
> (Heraclitus, 2001, p. 7)

Kingwell (1998) spelled out a profound difference between Descartes and Montaigne as the "two claimants for the title of the first truly modern philosopher" (p. x). He noted that "the generally acknowledged winner" is Descartes "whose brilliantly clear mathematical mind bent itself, with great success, to the task of achieving certainty by way of method" (p. x). On the other hand, Kingwell explained,

> humane and literate, sometimes loose and rambling, but always charming and wise, Montaigne is never sure and he is never finished. Where Descartes finds positive proof and solid answers, Montaigne finds only variable experience and further questions. One favors treatises full of cold reasoning, the other personal essays full of warm intimation. (p. x)

I'm on the side of Montaigne who wrote essays that I understand in the French etymology as attempts or tries. Montaigne wrote in order to question and explore, a kind of rambling ruminating that might lead somewhere or nowhere, and if nowhere, then for sure that too would be a good somewhere to have arrived. Today, we write our essays with a Cartesian confident hubris that questions have answers, and that a sufficiently rigorous quest will lead us to truth, and that we will recognize the truth. Montaigne motivates me to maintain an imaginative momentum in the amazing and magical momentousness of the moment, the immediate moment that needs no mediation. And so, with Montaigne, I maintain a meandering musing in citations and memories and poetry that flows with sagacious savouring.

A few years ago, I returned to Robert's Arm, Newfoundland, where I began my teaching career, and where I taught for two years. As the classroom teacher for grade seven, I taught a wide range of curricular subjects, including English, social studies, religious studies, physical education, and health. Those first two years of teaching represent a significant foundation for my subsequent practice as a teacher, both in school and university classrooms. When I returned for a school reunion, more than 25 years had slipped by like a midnight whisper. I met one of my former teaching colleagues who said, "What I remember most about you is the day you walked into the staffroom, and banged an armful of books down on the table, and declared, I refuse to devote my life to the Nicky Normores of the world." He laughed, and I chuckled. I didn't tell him that in the quarter century since I left Robert's Arm, I had not once remembered my proclamation of frustration about Nicky Normore. But with my colleague's words, I too remembered Nicky Normore, remembered how little he wanted to be in school, remembered how little he ever wrote or contributed or cared, remembered how exasperated I often was with his lack of willingness to participate in the classroom community. Nicky Normore didn't care about school. And I could do nothing to change his mind.

But what I find most intriguing about my colleague's recollection of my frustration with Nicky Normore is that whenever I have recalled my first two years of teaching, I have generally regarded myself quite heroically, at least in imagination. I have a few photographs of the time. I participated in winter carnivals and hikes and basketball tournaments and Christmas dramas. I remember myself in numerous guises as energetic, creative, diligent, and caring. But, of course, that is only part of the story, a version of the story. I forgot Nicky Normore, or at least I gave up trying to make sense of him in his stories, in my story.

Yoke

how would my life
be different

if

when Jesus said,
Take my yoke upon you,

I had heard,
Take my joke upon you?

I take words in the world
too literally.

like Yogi Ramacharaka
I need to learn
the science of breath

to breathe silence
the way words sing
in the spaces between
signs of the alphabet

how yug, yogi, yoke
are all joined
like a celestial joke
that pokes holes in the charades
of fakirs, mountebanks, and sleveens.

a wisdom-seeker takes up
the philosophy that yokes
jokes with the breadth
of life's breath, nothing less.

> So, as an educator, I ask, what have I given my heart to?
>
> Since mindfulness, of all things,
> is the ground of being,
> to speak one's true mind,
> and to keep things known
> in common, serves all being.
> (Heraclitus, 2001, p. 59)

Andrews (2006) asked: "so, what does make us happy?" She then responded to her question: "It's warm, caring relationships with other people. Happiness has been on the decline because we live in a cold, cutthroat, uncaring culture. Most of us have rarely experienced being truly, truly cared for" (p. 17). I went to Simon Fraser University a while ago to be an external examiner for a doctoral student who had written a dissertation about the need for love in schools. I arrived at SFU a little early and I sat in the concourse and drank coffee and began reading *Thirst*, a new book of poems by Oliver (2006) who is one of the most popular poets in the world. She is best known as a poet who writes evocatively about nature. But in *Thirst*, she writes about her living with grief after her partner of more than 40 years died. In the first line of the first poem, Oliver professes: "My work is loving the world" (p. 1). That is my work too.

Albom (1997) recounted the last days of a remarkable teacher. Albom studied in college with Morrie Schwartz, and 20 years later visits him on Tuesdays as the old man is living-dying with amyotrophic lateral sclerosis (ALS) or Lou Gehrig's disease. This is a narrative of teaching and learning and living and becoming. It impressed me distinctly as men's understanding of relationship and wisdom and how to live in the world. It is tender and touching—a tribute to the enduring lessons (enduring loves) of a good teacher and his responsive student. Albom explained:

> The last class of my old professor's life took place once a week in his house, by a window in the study where he could watch a small hibiscus plant shed its pink leaves. The class met on Tuesdays. It began after breakfast. The subject was The Meaning of Life. It was taught from experience. (p. 1)

What would school be like if we taught the curriculum of the Meaning of Life? In many ways, Morrie seems larger than life, more loving than most of us will ever let ourselves be, but I think Morrie insisted on seeing the world hopefully and lovingly and enthusiastically. Morrie advised Albom: "Remember what I said about finding a meaningful life? . . . . Devote yourself to loving others, devote yourself to your community around you, and devote yourself to creating something that gives you purpose and meaning" (Albom, 1997, p. 127).

Yo-Yo

I & you
the two most used
words in English

full of Buber's
tensile tension

in Spanish
I is yo
you is tú

I-you you-I I-I you-you yo-yo

yo-tú tú-yo yo-yo tú-tú I-I

I know you
you know me

the stranger within
the stranger without

all connected on a string
that knows the limits

of gravity, or at least
its seductive attraction

the constant challenge
of yo-yo tangles

common and idiosyncratic
DNA, in the mirror,
the conjunction AND

everything, all of us
entwined like vines

> So, as an educator, I ask, what have I given my heart to?

> All people ought to know themselves
> and everyone be wholly mindful.
> (Heraclitus, 2001, p. 71)

Cohen (2006) sings his longing, an old man's song of praise and lament. Cohen has lived enough of the world's challenges and privileges to have some wisdom to offer. He advises us to "press your lips/to the light of my heart" (p. 120). At the heart of light is an ongoing practice of story-making. As we share with one another our stories, all our stories, we grow in wisdom and intimacy and joy. We can tell our true stories and we can tell them truthfully, and in turn we can testify to the joyfulness that holds us fast. Baldwin (2005) reminded us that "it takes courage to tell our stories" (p. 18). We need to hear one another's stories. We need to embrace the healing efficacy of sharing stories. Baldwin understood that "when we reveal details that we think are excruciatingly personal, we discover that the personal is universal" (p. 85). My story is your story; your story is my story. Yet, as W. Berry (1990) knew,

> most of us no longer talk with each other, much less tell each other stories. We tell our stories now mostly to doctors or lawyers or psychiatrists or insurance adjusters or the police, not to our neighbors for their (and our) entertainment. The stories that now entertain us are made up for us in New York or Los Angeles or other centers of such commerce. (p. 159)

Larimar
(for Lana)

the other morning
I stepped out of the shower
in a typical rush to leave,
and you swept into the room,

just risen from bed
in a nightie like larimar,
with hair tousled, a glad smile,
offering a kiss good morning,
and I heard the ceiling fan
like echoes of the sea faraway
on Dominican beaches

another morning soon after
you stepped out of the shower
wearing only a scar
(a cyst doctors insisted
was cancer, driven out
by steadfast imagination)
and a small silver cross
on a chain like a lariat
you wound around my neck
like a gentle noose, more
beautiful even than that day

we first knew each other
when only thirteen
(surely if any are lucky,
this is a lucky number)

how the familiar so
readily, steadily surprises
(four decades can be held
only gratefully in a poem)

legend contends larimar
heals, helps us see
events with wisdom
like the light Caribbean Sea
washes us from the inside out

So, as an educator, I ask, what have I given my heart to?

The ape apes find
most beautiful
looks apish
to non-apes.
(Heraclitus, 2001, p. 65)

Buechner (2006) wrote that "the world is full of darkness, but . . . at the heart of darkness . . . there is joy unimaginable" (p. 240). That is the story we need to share with one another and with others. I recommend that educators practice belly laughs. (I suspect that belly dancing would be useful, too, but that's a theme to be addressed elsewhere.) Educators need to cultivate joy, to engage in a daily practice of seeking and acknowledging and promoting joy. Andrews (2006) doesn't mince words in her observation: "Judgmental people don't laugh. Rigid moralists don't laugh. Extremists don't laugh. Most right-wingers have phony smiles and wooden faces. They are rigid, uncompassionate automatons. Demagogues and dictators don't have a sense of humor" (pp. 129-130). Do educators have a sense of humour?

Love in the Time of Scholars

Scholars vie with one another like eager contestants on
The Price is Right or Make a Deal or American Idol,
Simon Cowell's grimace as fierce as an unpopular dean's.

Scholars travel by boat, bus, bicycle, car, limousine,
plane, scooter, taxi, train, truck, van, round and round,
mesmerized at conferences here and there, everywhere.

Scholars perform acrobatics like the Cirque du Soleil,
pudgy round academics in sequined leotards
discussing the gymnastic turns of Jean-François Lyotard.

Scholars always look like they need to be someplace
else, are always looking for important people,
at least people more important than you and me.

Scholars talk loudly on cell phones and Blackberries
like they want everybody to hear their business,
like the future of Iraq or Nasdaq depends on them.

Scholars complain always about the lack
of academic rigour, like Hugh Hefner, dreaming
of Viagra, sleepless with fears of erectile dysfunction.

Scholars jostle like guppies around the pastry table,
voracious for cinnamon buns, blueberry scones,
bran muffins, sugar cookies, and coconut squares.

Scholars shuffle through the Sheraton like zombies
mesmerized with loss or hope, zombies on Zambonis,
slow moves around the slick marble floor.

Scholars carry business cards in platinum cases
like Humphrey Bogart carried cigarettes,
pushing cards like a Fuller Brush Man.

Scholars bump one another with stuffed backpacks
like bumper cars, ramble and rumble, a desiccated cliché
in a single key, words worn out with asthmatic puffing.

Scholars present powerful points with Powerpoint,
wielding technology with a magician's
eager stealth for keeping the earth spinning.

Scholars hold words with fundamentalist zeal,
wrestle words with a choke hold, claim they want
to be mentors, but really want mini-me mentees.

Scholars need poetry, especially amidst the maze
of e-mail, meetings, and memos marked urgent, though
the only urgency is the lovely lie that never lies still.

> So, as an educator, I ask, what have I given my heart to?

> People dull their wits with gibberish,
> and cannot use their ears and eyes.
> (Heraclitus, 2001, p. 5)

I agree with Coffin (2004) that "we have lost our sense of wonder" (p. 113). So, I often invite my students in writing classes to "wander for wonder." We leave the classroom, and we stroll around campus, stopping to get up close and personal with a tree or to listen to the grass or to taste the cherry blossoms. Andrews (2006) recommended that "approaching life with wonder means that we try to keep alive the feeling that life is wonderful—to never feel that we have the final answer, but to keep searching and to experience a connectedness with the whole" (p. 152). In our wandering for wonder, we are seeking T. Berry's (2000) wisdom: "the universe is composed of subjects to be communed with, not objects to be exploited. Every mode of being has its own inner spontaneity, its capacity to evoke wonder and praise from every other being" (p. 36).

Twelve Riffs for a Guitar with No Strings

1

I once saw the full moon pinned
just over the Empire State Building,

a circle like God's mouth, an O full
of surprise.

2

I will write as if no one will ever read
my poems; I will not write for others
because I will be too eager to please.

3

I just finished breakfast in IHOP,
and I am caffeinated, content, and contained,
like I imagine the Cleaver family spends
their days after the TV is turned off.

4

I hear the languages of winter, especially
steeped mint tea on a windswept day,
and try to translate what I hear
like love letters that never arrive.

5

Like electrical circuits
my nerve endings are overloaded.
So many tales full of details,
my life wagged by the tails in details.

6

I cannot eat all the foods I want,
or read all the books I want,
or write all the poems I want,
or count all the ways of love I want.

7

I am facing the loss of my myths,
dangerous, like losing mitts in winter
where survival depends on warm words.

8

Once taut, steeled with wise words,
I am broken, empty, full of fear,
like living in a radioactive zone after a spill.

9

On my back in the Caribbean Sea,
suspended in salt waves, the sky is
a hallowed hollow where I will fall
unless I cling to the memory of you.

10

She told the hair stylist, Dye
the blond streaks out of my hair.
Why did you get streaks?
I was going through a bad time.
The hair stylist said, Our hair
bears the heart's story.

11

Before Valerie died, she reminded me
how I once advised her, Learn to sit
for an hour on a bench and do nothing,
and know love is the answer to all
the questions. Good advice, even
if I don't practice it.

12

Seagulls carry mussels and sea urchins
in land from the edge of the ocean
and drop them on rocks for a picnic
like I need to break my poems open.

> So, as an educator, I ask, what have I given my heart to?

> Stupidity is doomed,
> therefore, to cringe
> at every syllable
> of wisdom.
> (Heraclitus, 2001, p. 81)

According to Davis (2002), "a year 2000 study from the University of California at Berkeley's School of Information Management and Systems concludes that the world is now producing 2 exabytes of new and unique information per year" (p. 54). She further explained that "an exabyte is a billion gigabytes" (p. 54). Now, I don't really know what a gigabyte is, but a billion of them sounds like a lot! We live in an Information Age. We live in the age of the Internet and Google and Wikipedia and Facebook and e-mail and blogging. We are immersed in information, but how much do we know? I have a lot of university degrees, and I've read a lot of books, but I don't know very much. At least I know that much. What I really know is that the universe is much bigger and far more mysterious than I will ever be able to fathom or ascertain.

Above all, I resonate with W. Berry's (2001) perspective that

> education is not properly an industry, and its proper use is not to serve industries, either by job-training or by industry-subsidized research. Its proper use is to enable citizens to live lives that are economically, politically, socially, and culturally responsible. This cannot be done by gathering or 'accessing' what we now call 'information'—which is to say facts without context and therefore without priority. (p. 9)

But in spite of my beliefs and convictions, I still often ask if I am just a cog in the intricately lumbering machinery of the institution, one more widget-tightening, drone-like citizen in a factory that serves the memory of Henry Ford with diligent devotion and a lifetime of exasperated, silenced sighs. In order to seek wisdom, I need to be committed daily, even moment by moment, to challenging the conceits and claims of the Information Age with an educator's calling to an ancient wisdom that resonates with hope for a Transformation Age.

During one of our snowy days this past winter, I was hoping that UBC would be closed, but it wasn't, and so I drove to campus in an early morning snowstorm, just a whisker short of danger, upset with administrators who did not seem to care about the safety of others, and as I successfully navigated the serpentine route along southwest Marine Drive, I arrived on campus amidst trees hidden in sun-soaked snow. Then, a little later, sitting at my desk, I saw outside my office window a sparrow in the branch of an alder tree I didn't even know was there, and I was overwhelmed with a sense of the sumptuous gorgeousness, and the miraculous ordinariness all around me.

Light Echoes

I jam with the wild lunacy
of the wind tangled in alders,
the day's light in the aspens

&
silence spilled in the forest's arteries
spells the heart's endless desire

&
located in the earth, I will learn
to keep the heart calling earth's rhythms
with roots seeking deep and deeper,
the whole earth sung in veins of long light

&
as the sun falls lower and lower,
the sun chants and I chant with the sun
in ancient blood rhythms

&
in the whirligig of wild imaginings
I breathe raucous ramblings with no anchor point
like a deflating balloon that never runs out of air

&
the lyrical light fall of rain remembers
the morning star in a heather-blue sky

&
these rhythms are the flow of blood,
breath, breathing, breath-giving,
the measure of the heart, knowing
the living word to inspirit hope, even
in the midst of each day's chaos

> So, as an educator, I ask, what have I given my heart to?

> The harmony past knowing sounds
> more deeply than the known.
> (Heraclitus, 2001, p. 31)

In a remarkable memoir, Bauby (1997) recounted the year after a stroke rendered his body paralyzed except for one eye that he could still blink. He dictates his memoir by blinking this one eye in response to a secretary who calls out the letters of the alphabet. Bauby blinks his eye when the secretary speaks the letter he wants. Like laying stones in a long, high wall, Bauby narrates his memories, desires, regrets, and fears, one letter at a time, one blink at a time. In his hospital bed, alone, silent, immobile, Bauby observed:

> I can listen to the butterflies that flutter inside my head. To hear them, one must be calm and pay close attention, for their wingbeats are barely audible. Loud breathing is enough to drown them out. This is astonishing: my hearing

does not improve, yet I hear them better and better. I must have the ear of a butterfly. (pp. 104–105)

Imagine a pedagogy of listening and attending so we could hear the wingbeats of butterflies.

Resonance

another summer day on Lomond Street,
on the Verge patio, where I have lazed
often during obligatory August visits,
wondering if the crows will eat
all the cherries before somebody climbs
a ladder to pick a bucket nobody wants.

for a few moments I am lost
in keen still nothing till
a Skipper butterfly pulls past, full
of purpose, and drops into the spruce
I haven't seen for a long time.

the butterfly works hard to navigate
the still air like molasses, makes
a sudden brief appearance, startles
me, present for a moment, then gone.

we live in an affluent age, an effluent age
where we are always throwing things away
except nothing is ever really discarded.
the plastic cup I hold will outlast me
by a century at least, probably longer.

and now the world has changed because
a butterfly lighted in the spruce I haven't seen
for a long time while I thought about
unwanted cherries and watched Peggy
next door leaning into her garden.

So, as an educator, I ask, what have I given my heart to?

> The rule that makes
> its subject weary
> is a sentence
> of hard labor.
> (Heraclitus, 2001, p. 53)

Calvino (1995) spelled out the need for a "pedagogy of the imagination" (p. 92). In the supple prose that marks all of Calvino's wise writing, he proposed:

> Were I to choose an auspicious image for the new millennium, I would choose . . . the sudden agile leap of the poet-philosopher who raises himself above the weight of the world, showing that with all his gravity he has the secret of lightness, and that what many consider to be the vitality of the times—noisy, aggressive, revving and roaring—belongs to the realm of death, like a cemetery for rusty old cars. (p. 12)

Calvino expanded at length on his theme of lightness, and I only intend here to open a crack so a little light can begin to seep in. Like Calvino, W. Berry (2001) observed that "we are involved now in a profound failure of imagination" (p. 40). How does education dictate against lightness and imagination? Berry offered an important and unsettling perspective:

> The law of competition is a simple paradox: Competition destroys competition. The law of competition implies that many competitors, competing without restraint, will ultimately and inevitably reduce the number of competitors to one. The law of competition, in short, is the law of war. (p. 20)

I have lived all my life in school, and all my life has been governed by competition. That is a sad confession. I remember in elementary school that Herbert, my best friend, and I were often awarded first and second places in our class at the end of the year. One year, Herbert would be first, and I would be second, and the next year, we switched places. We went back and forth like that for several years. Then, in grade five, I was awarded first place based on a total accumulation of marks that was one percentage point more than Herbert's. I remember distinctly thinking that I would be happier if Herbert and I had tied. I felt a hollowness at the heart of my sanctioned success. That moment was a kind of ethical stopping station for me. I received the first place prize, and Herbert received the second place prize. In the subsequent years, our competition continued, but now with more fervour, at least on my part. I don't think Herbert ever came first again. All my life has been lived competitively, and I agree with Berry that "the law of competition . . . is the law of war" (p. 20). Sometimes, I interrogate with my students the valorization of the letter A in evaluation. I recommend that we might give Z instead. But, of course, the problem does not lie in the letter itself, which, after all, is only a signifier that can be invested with many meanings. The problem lies in our evaluation policies and practices where we interpret value (the root of evaluation) in measurable, standard, competitive ways that always guarantee many learners will feel the crack of the yardstick on their backs.

Blue Star

on a January morning
Tommy Samson challenged
Cec, Frazer, Macky,
my brother and me

to a test of manhood;
one who keeps his hands
in snow longest wins
a medal, promised
Tommy Samson who packed
snow into the holes
our hot hands melted,
and Frazer gave up
quickly as he always did
and Cec had to go
to the store for his mother
and Macky who wanted
licorice went with Cec
and my brother heard
my eyes shout,
Chop my hands off
before I give up,
and went home
to watch T.V.
(he didn't like
beating me anyway),
and my hands were mottled
pink blue white like opal
when Tommy Samson
carefully removed
the cork liner
from a Blue Star
beer bottle cap
and slipped a fiery hand
inside my shirt
to press the liner
against the cotton
into the cap held
on the outside,
to pinch the medal
in place over my heart,
the only medal I won
from Tommy Samson
because in the spring
he fell off the log boom
in Deer Lake and drowned,
but years later
I'm still competing
for Blue Star medals

    So, as an educator, I ask, what have I given my heart to?

> The cosmos works
> by harmony of tensions,
> like the lyre and bow.
> (Heraclitus, 2001, p. 37)

I recently read a book that is changing my middle-aged ways of being in the world. Vienne and Lennard (1999) remind me that imperfection is everywhere, all the time. With references to complexity theory they boldly claim that "it is the sum total of our mistakes—which is also called experience—that allows us to learn from, adapt to, and ultimately survive in the most unexpected and challenging conditions" (pp. 70–71). Moreover, they call for "practicing generosity of spirit" (p. 89). That's the kind of wisdom I need. As part of their defense of the art of imperfection, Vienne and Lennard also refer to flaws in Islamic art, music, and literature, as well as the Zen tradition of "'wabi-sabi' objects, carefully crafted to be intentionally imperfect, impermanent, or incomplete" (p. 17).

So, inspired by Vienne and Lennard's art of imperfection, I acknowledge that this paper might be better if I hadn't gone for a walk with my daughter Anna and granddaughter Madeleine and Mr. Burns, our bassett hound. Of course, perhaps it would be a lot worse if I hadn't gone for the walk, and had stayed home and read another book or wrote another hundred words. All I know is that this paper is full of flaws and cracks and bumps—just like me. And I am finally learning to rest with the imperfections, always in humane and heartful hope.

Mr. Burns Teaches Ecology

My boots are muddy
from hikes on the dike
with Mr. Burns

who reminds me
that everything
is worth studying:

the blackberry brambles
that horde their purple hearts
with sensible jealousy

the wet brown grass curled
around the sign posts like
malnourished garter snakes

the ducks in the slough
laughing to one another
with their funniest stories.

Mr. Burns keeps his nose
close to the ground as though
he is myopic, but really

he just wants to be near
the earth, catching the story's
scent with his big ears.

> The beginning is the end.
> (Heraclitus, 2001, p. 45)

And surely the end is the beginning. That, then, is what I have given my heart to.

REFERENCES

Akenson, D. H. (1998). *Surpassing wonder: The invention of the Bible and the Talmuds*. Montreal & Kingston: McGill-Queen's University Press.
Albom, M. (1997). *Tuesdays with Morrie*. New York: Doubleday.
Andrews, C. (2006). *Slow is beautiful: New visions of community, leisure and joie de vivre*. Gabriola Island: New Society Publishers.
Baldwin, C. (2005). *Storycatcher: Making sense of our lives through the power and practice of story*. Novato: New World Library.
Bauby, J. (1997). *The diving-bell and the butterfly* (J. Leggatt, Trans.). London: Harper Perennial.
Berry, T. (2000). In F. Franck, J. Roze, & R. Connolly (Eds.), *What does it mean to be human?* (pp. 32–38). New York: St. Martin's Press.
Berry, W. (2001). *In the presence of fear: Three essays for a changed world*. Great Barrington: The Orion Society.
Berry, W. (1990). *What are people for? Essays*. New York: North Point Press.
Buechner, F. (2006). *Secrets in the dark: A life in sermons*. New York: HarperCollins.
Calvino, I. (1995). *Six memos for the next millennium*. Toronto: Vintage Canada.
Coffin, W. S. (2004). *Credo*. Louisville: Westminster John Knox Press.
Cohen, L. (2006). *Book of longing*. Toronto: McClelland & Stewart.
Davis, M. (2002). *The new culture of desire*. New York: The Free Press.
Freire, P. (1993). *Pedagogy of the city* (D. Macedo, Trans.). New York: Continuum.
Heraclitus. (2001). *Fragments* (B. Haxton, Trans.). New York: Penguin.
Kingwell, M. (1998). *In pursuit of happiness*. New York: Crown Publishers.
Oliver, M. (2006). *Thirst*. Boston: Beacon Press.
Vienne, V., & Lennard, E. (1999). *The art of imperfection: Simple ways to make peace with yourself*. New York: Clarkson Potter.
Woodruff, P. (2001). *Reverence: Renewing a forgotten virtue*. Oxford: Oxford University Press.

INNERWORKINGS

KAREN MEYER

LIVING INQUIRY

I fell in love in a bookstore . . .

LIVING INQUIRY

A Splinter and a Book

I fell in love in a bookstore. Psychedelic posters, Persian rugs and tie-dye curtains fashioned its eclectic, artsy aura. A thick and strangely sweet smoke in the air left an exotic taste in my mouth impossible to forget. I was barely in my twenties and looking for something to read that would justify or just explain my restlessness about pretty much everything. High school had been a complete bust, stuck inside clichéd textbooks that dodged any scent of controversy. Even now, I can picture my wide-eyed self—brimmed hat, long skirt, Rasta-coloured scarf, and macramé shoulder bag—rummaging through the shelves of books pressed spine to spine, stowaway words and worlds, flesh and blood, in wait for one rupture, one chance to spill from the gut. Much like me. My anxious mood was akin to what Morpheus describes to Neo in the film The Matrix (1997): "It's that feeling you have had all your life. That feeling that something was wrong with the world. You don't know what it is but it's there, like a splinter in your mind." I was searching for my own Morpheus in that tiny bookstore, my own guru with some answers.

One book caught my attention, *The Awakening of Intelligence* written by Jiddu Krishnamurti (1973). I recall my attraction to the cover photo of this Indian man not posing but looking like he was saying something worth hearing. His hands were lifted off his lap and his eyes were fixed yet serene. His dark skin stood out against his grey hair and light coloured clothing. I liked his name. I immediately began wading, thumbing, and skimming through the pages. What hit me right away was Krishnamurti's intense appeal to see everyday life as it is without preferences and attachments, and to observe the whole movement of life with fresh eyes. He insisted we are severely conditioned, calling us second hand human beings. I was love-struck!

The more I read, the more I felt understood. The book lived with me for months. Everyday I entered the text, inserting my self between its lines. Faded playing cards flagged particular pages, a joker here, queen of hearts there. Pencil marks underlined words. My hand-written thoughts flooded the margins with big question marks hanging in the borders like hooks waiting for a catch I could reel in. Tea and chocolate stains blemished the wrinkled, dog-eared pages. And the cover with K-man's photo was worn having been opened and closed so many times. For a spell the book and I were inseparable. But, somewhere along the path we parted ways. Like a true first love, the book vanished. I'm not sure where. Like me, it got lost somewhere in the world of 'they' and 'things.'

The second time I bought the book, I was in my early thirties and attending college part time because I had a job and two young kids. This time school wasn't a complete bust but not what I imagined education could be. It was fragmented into disciplines and knowledge bits for students to swallow up in mega quantities.

Cramming for exams was like knowledge eating contests. We sat at desks, stuffed ourselves until we could hold no more, and then regurgitated at the exam. The splinter in my mind was there still re-minding me that something was amiss in the world. K-man's book sat on my bookshelf like a dependable antidote to be read as needed. The message was simple: 'wake up.'

A few years later, the book vanished again. I gave it away following a lively conversation with a musician I met. I suspect it was my idea he should read the book. Both disappeared. By then I was a teacher and graduate student. Education and writing found significance in my life. Even so, what I studied felt disconnected to my life as a woman, mother, and teacher.

I did buy the book a third time, close to 30 years after first finding it in that tiny, artsy bookstore that smelled of incense. This story of the book as soul mate speaks to my enduring interest in awareness and practicing what it means to see the world as it is. At that time I was teaching at a university. While in an administrative position, I developed a course I named 'Living Inquiry.' I designed it to study, as intimate practice, how we participate in the structure, content, and movement of daily life, how we experience our inner and outer worldliness in everyday living. Krishnamurti (1973) called such awareness 'intelligence,' when the mind becomes highly active and sensitive to what it's doing, what goes on in daily life, and what happens in times of inattention (when we are occupied in brain clutter). Given the diversity of my students' backgrounds, cultures, and languages, my hunch was that stepping into individual and shared narratives, histories, and realities into which they were born and live would make a worthy curriculum. I began writing about my own practice of Living Inquiry (Meyer, 2010; 2006).

I've taught Living Inquiry many times with graduate students, practicing inner-city teachers and with students at an elementary school. To start the course, we engage several themes to spark inquiry and our field notes: place, language, time and self/other (including non-human other). Attention to place grounds my body and heightens sensitivity to the surrounding physical and social textures. I need only ask, where am I? Place is where I go, where I find myself, where I live and belong. It is home; it is exile. Attention to language unveils its omnipresent nature as the medium in which I think, express myself, and interpret the actions and utterances of others. Language holds traditions, stories, and histories. It is political as well as poetic. The infinity of the unsaid lives in language. Time tells me about the temporality and finitude of my life. In a given moment, time can appear on the horizon as ahead-of-itself, present, or as having been. Time isn't as reliable as clockwork—sometimes it beats true and steady, other times it tics according to my mood and circumstance. Time eludes. And finally, self/other as a theme has an innermost edge since each of us is at once both self and other. I share the sameness of being human and experience the difference of being unique. My discriminations toward other are more clear when I see how I see others. Somewhere along these beginning lines of inquiry, the themes fade into the background as I keep moving my practice deeper into what is daily life.

Field notes support the practice of Living Inquiry. They document events of understanding inside everyday anecdotes. Creating field notes (as texts, art forms or performances) bring lived experience close as I listen to being-there. When students share their field notes with others in the class, another level of inquiry emerges—witnesses listening and attending to the lived experience of others.

In one class I recall joining students in the throes of an intense discussion sparked by an abstract painting one student shared as a weekly field note. In the painting there was an infinity symbol at the top of a large circular motif. Group members were debating whether or not time begins and ends. The spirited and sophisticated discussion covered topics related to life, God, death, birth, scientism, and the universe. We listened to each voice, sometimes many at a time until a bell interrupted, signalling the end of time, that is, the end of the school day. At that moment, I realized I had totally forgotten I was in an elementary school among grade seven students. That discussion was a highlight in my teaching life.

In my own practice, my field notes are texts. They aren't journal writings or free writings. I don't write them every day. I craft and polish them over many days. I listen to them in rough form, take out anything superfluous, and hold onto only what matters, what is the essence, what is poetic. This writing process sustains my inner and outer lines of inquiry, as I try to loosen the splinter still lodged in my mind.

Below is a field note from my collection, As The Crow Flies. In this experience, seeing the nature of Crow inspired an insight about potential and its edge. A Closer Look follows. I wrote this narrative from extensive field notes and a truant practice of sitting on a tiny beach for a string of days, living like there was no tomorrow, and taking a closer look at what goes on in the daily life of a place.

FIELD NOTE: AS THE CROW FLIES

> Young Crow lands in a most awkward manner. Not easy to put down on such a narrow space, halfway up a high-rise. Seems Crow's in a spot—my balcony, but not my place to interfere. We are two unlikely characters sharing an in-between place. Two crows circle the sky close-by. I hear insistence not panic in their calls. Crow paces. From the looks of things my companion is learning to fly. The correct movement will catch a lift with wind and another short flight. Crow stands on the ledge that stands high in the city. Like me Crow is urban. From a bird's-eye view the landscape looks like a circuit board made up of tall concrete and glass components and connecting corridors that conduct the city's flow. Now is the essential moment at that edge before take off, when all potential comes into being. Crow flies and my attention stands still as if next is my turn.

REFERENCES

Krishnamurti, J. (1973). *The awakening of intelligence*. San Francisco: HarperCollins.
Meyer, K. (2010) Living inquiry: Me, myself and other. *Journal of Curriculum Theorizing, 26*(1), 85–96.
Meyer, K. (2006). Living inquiry: A gateless gate and a beach, In W. Ashton and D. Denton (eds.) *Spirituality, Ethnography, and Teaching: Stories from Within*. New York: Peter Lang.
Wachowski, L. & Wachowski, A. (1997). Matrix: Screenplay by the Wachowski Brothers. Warner Brothers Entertainment.

A CLOSER LOOK

I found my grandmother's notebook packed away in a cardboard box labeled 'old photographs.' It was worn, having been opened and closed so many times by my grandmother's hands. Once upon a time its cover was pristine buff leather and its pages white. When I opened the frayed cover and saw the first page, I recognized the curves of my grandmother's handwriting in the same way I would recognize the tone of her voice if I heard it again. Her words, handwritten or spoken, always sounded practical and genuine like the character she was. Barbara Edith. Over tea at my mother's kitchen table, I stepped into the world of my grandmother's notebook for a closer look.

The notebook was not a diary. It was a list of events and dates: the death of her mother and young son, my mother's birth, my wedding, my son's birth. Each entry loosened fragments of stories I barely remembered or could only imagine. Page by page, the lists kept a faithful account of a family, back and forth across five generations. The order was not chronological. Rather, it was timely— whenever Barbara opened her notebook she added significant events to the lists, perhaps whatever she could recall at that moment. My grandmother told me time and again to write important things down lest they be forgotten.

My list begins on the back of a used envelope, well-traveled and torn open from one end to the other. It sits on my kitchen table reminding me, as Barbara would, of practical things I need to do and pack. My handwriting is legible but hurried and cursory, which sums up my life at the moment, running from one thing to the next without ever feeling caught up. The list becomes longer and messier by the day. New scrawls on scraps of paper keep showing up on the kitchen table. Lord, more to do and pack. I have written down some essentials, what first comes to mind for a list of this sort: things to take along for living a season on an island off the coast of British Columbia during my sabbatical from teaching.

I'm not sure why my lists never warrant a clean sheet of paper. Maybe because I know they'll only end up as remnants in my pockets, or scraps at the bottom of shopping bags, or shreds of paper folded and slipped into my wallet for safekeeping, but then forgotten. The noun 'list' originally meant border or edging, a selvage of fabric, a strip. Likewise, my lists turn up on the edges of things, on the verge of being important.

By now the collection of belongings and provisions I cannot do without waits by my apartment door. What's missing? What haven't I remembered, considered, imagined? What I take with me will have to sustain me for my months of seclusion in a modest cottage on the edge of the sea. I am going there to write about what I do.

I teach. I've decided I have a few important things to say about it. During this sabbatical, I will write them down. Not as lists. As full-fledged stories that matter to a teacher's life. Lest they be forgotten.

But what will inspire me to write? Shall I bring something beautiful? Something old, something new? Borrowed, blue? Shall I bring practical things? I want to feel comfortable, feel at home. Shall I keep life simple, half naked? Push myself to the edge of have and have not? Suffer as a writer should? What I've collected has to fit in my compact car.

Before I leave, I carefully choose a notebook, with a plain brown moleskin cover, to write things down—events of my life on a small island. I've heard that's what writers do. They keep notebooks. Who knows what can happen on an island. I head off for the first of two ferries and the short drive up island to the cottage.

> Belongings are the intimacies we carry with us,
> too special to part with.

* * * *

Because the lists in my grandmother's notebook made me curious, I asked my mother about the details. As a young woman, Barbara left the family farm near a small Canadian prairie town for Chicago in the 1920s. She must have left behind familiarity, family, friends that moulded her life. I imagine Barbara, not yet 20, standing on the weathered, wooden platform outside the station, under overhanging eaves, waiting for the train, looking already lost—brimmed hat, overcoat, wool scarf, leather suitcase in each hand. What belongings did she pack in her bags for her new life as a nanny? What did she choose to bring along to ease distant feelings inside a new family home in a large American city? When did a place become home for Barbara? What went on in the interim, in the meanwhile, in the between times? These questions stir my own memories of moving to Canada in my thirties and crossing that same border.

I drive across the steel ramp onto the Queen of Nanaimo and park on the tail of the car ahead. We all pack in the ferry like sardines in a can. The smell of car exhaust makes me lightheaded. Later a steady beat of heavy metal clunks as cars exit the ramp. This trip to Vancouver Island is the first leg of my journey. From Nanaimo I will take a second, smaller ferry for a short trip to an island only 14 kilometres long and four kilometres wide. Now called Gabriola, the island was named Gaviota, the Spanish word for gull, by a Spanish explorer in the late 1700s. I have a feeling that Gabriola by any other name would be just as sweet.

Traveling by ferry is slow. I will walk around the deck, own the time between parting and arriving. I will daydream about being lost at sea on my sabbatical from teaching.

When I was a kid my family took several road trips in a 1961 cream coloured six-cylinder Chevy station wagon. One word: Disaster. My sincerest sympathies go to my parents. The events of those long taxing drives, the 'getting there,' spin over and over in 'funny' family yarns: when I was carsick on my father's back while he was driving; when my father lit the heater in the borrowed trailer and singed his eyebrows in the explosion; when three adults, three kids, and a dog drove the Chevy 'straight through,' 2,350 kilometres in dead winter, to my great-grandmother's house, ending in a shallow ditch in the last hundred metres while my great-grandmother, who had watched us approach, said to her husband Sam, "They just disappeared."

For me, travel was a means to an end. I always embodied restlessness, jumping ahead in time, asking my parents how soon we would get there. How long would it be before I realized it is the taxiing between events and places that constitute a life. The running between one thing and the next.

Once on board the ferry I leave the confinement of my crowded car and join the other passengers as they scurry to the upper levels, the window seats inside, the deck seats outside, and the cafeteria that leaks fried food aromas across the entire level. Squeezing past the rows of tightly parked cars lets me see backseats filled up with boxes and suitcases. Ferries are the main transport between the islands and the mainland for commuters, full-time islanders, and visitors alike. You can spot the local islanders by their casual attire in colourful combinations. Comfort and function trump fashion. Locals live a slower, saner pace, disconnected from the mainland matrix. Fewer wear cell phones and headphones. Many are retired. And me? I've traded my busy urban life to stand on a windy deck aboard the Queen of Nanaimo—brimmed hat, denim jacket, wool scarf, backpack.

* * * *

I learned the ritual of unpacking and settling in from Friday arrivals at my grandparents' cabin in southern California. Sometimes it was best to stay clear of the three adults when we first got there. During the three-hour trip from home in my grandfather's blue 1954 Ford Mainliner two-door sedan, they'd had enough of us three kids fighting in the backseat. Yes, best to tag along with my big brother and his BB gun into the bush, while my grandparents and mother unloaded the car.

Then the ritual would begin. My grandmother and mother would head inside to put things away, make the beds, start dinner. I would follow my grandfather around on his outside routine, stamping his Camel cigarettes into the ground, sneaking sips of beer when he set down his can of Lucky Lager. First, he would turn on the propane tank that powered the one-room cabin. Then, I would chatter after him, keeping the long green hose untangled as he walked around the cabin watering the young trees he'd planted a few years back and filling the tiny ponds he'd built for the animals in this dry climate; save the rattler, who showed up one day and caused quite a ruckus. I'd help my grandfather rake the horseshoe pit, empty the coffee cans set in the ground for croquette, and put out the patio furniture and picnic table for the Friday evening poker game. Later, I would pretend to be asleep on a cot in the patio and listen to the adult jokes over the clacking of plastic poker chips.

The rituals that were part of arrival were my favourite parts of those weekends, the joy of doing practical things, doing what needs to be done. Belonging with a family in a home away from home.

When I arrive at the cottage I start unloading the car, bringing what I can carry to the front porch. I scan the yard with each back and forth trip, arms full. Off to the right I notice a cord of wood covered with a blue tarp, a chopping block, axe, ready to go. A new experience of splitting wood awaits me. There's a small shanty, trailer size, on the front of the property, a lawn full of tiny daisies, a dozen evergreens taller than I can see, a few deciduous trees. No sign of the sea from here, but I can smell salt water in the air. I know there's an ocean view somewhere. The owner e-mailed me photos.

I feel a quick chaotic quiver from head to toe as I open the front door. I want to get started, do what needs to be done. The ritual begins in this full moment. I am here, ready to settle in, already wondering when this place will feel like home, when the smell of strangeness will succumb to familiar scents—my teas, my cooking, my body. The entryway's dark paneling is the first thing I see, then the dead cuckoo clock frozen on its perch half way outside its house. I walk through the front of the cottage, down the hallway into the kitchen and spot another stopped clock on the wall. I continue to the bathroom and then the two bedrooms for a closer look, like a scout sent ahead to gather information, survey the landscape.

This layout will be the pathway I trek every day, and blindly in the middle of the night. My neural pathways, set for my apartment, will adapt. I walk another round through this part of the cottage. More paneling. Eclectic décor and furnishings, bent on staying, compete for space and shout early casual 1960s, cottage-like, colourful combinations. Comfort and function trump contemporary style. I see démodé sofas covered with wool blankets from Latin America; wooden, stuffed, and reclining chairs; pottery and knickknack galore; prints on the walls from Picasso to Haida art. Wall hangings from Latin America.

Nothing has changed here for decades. The living/dining area, the front focus of this cottage when it was a full-time home a generation ago, doesn't appear to be the main living space for the family that now summers here. This part of the cottage faces north.

Beyond the dining room I see sliding glass doors facing south, exploding in afternoon sun. With a moth's compulsion, I walk toward the light. Now I see why the front of the house facing north has been abandoned.

This room spans the entire width of the cottage with full length windows facing the sea. A moth's Nirvana or have I just boarded a ship? The strip of grass on the other side of the windows could be the deck with Arbutus trees leaning over the bow gobbling up sunlight reflected by the sea. On a stormy day would I feel the rolling motion of a heavy swell? Across a narrow channel, a little lighthouse flashes red with its own particular rhythm. There are other small islands in the distance and a tiny beach below the stern to the right.

The two side walls also have windows. This glass rectangular box was once the patio. Now it is a 12-metre-long room big enough for a dining table, and a sitting area with sofas, chairs and a wood stove, all in front of the sea of windows. From these south-facing windows I will see the sky move from east to west, water and light dancing night and day.

So this is where the summer family hangs out, in the space I later learn they call the 'Gabriola Room.' The original rooms of the cottage—a bedroom, the kitchen and dining room—now have windows or sliding glass doors opening onto the Gabriola Room. The sea is visible from the bed, the kitchen sink, the dining room. Windows everywhere.

While checking things out, I find a scrapbook, much like my grandmother's notebook, tucked away on a bookshelf with books about animals of British Columbia. From photos and bits of text, I learn that the cottage is 40 years old. It was built as a retirement home by Fred and Sally, who would live here for 23 years. Fred built the shanty first back by the road, then the cottage. Photos document the process. Here is Sally hanging up clothes on an unfinished deck, turning to wave at the camera. Here is Fred labouring away at the construction site, looking up to grin. A handwritten caption below one photo of the cottage reads "The retirement home complete!" Is this Sally's handwriting? Neat and careful. Fred and Sally, like my grandmother, were from a generation who wrote things down, kept photos.

The cottage is about 12 by eight metres. I imagine Sally daydreaming out the kitchen window. The floor plan, included in the scrapbook, is the Centennial II designed by Holiday Homes—"built better to last longer." I learned about floor plans from buying my apartment in Vancouver and thinking about ways to maximize space. This plan is efficient. The accompanying description, written in the early 1960s, markets the role as homemaker:

> Here the lady of the house will marvel at the large, family-size kitchen, cabinets galore and adjacent to the kitchen is a plus from Holiday Homes Ltd., a Utility Room for your washer and dryer, no need to wear yourself out in this house, it has been designed to save you steps.

The lady of the house is now the writer of the house. With a room of her own. A room with a view.

Arrivals end with beginnings.

* * * *

I count five sofas and a dozen chairs. People must sit a lot in cottages, extended family, visitors. I have put away my belongings, set up the drum kit I'm learning to play so it faces the Omnimax windows. But my most critical task is still undone. The house may have cabinets galore and a handy utility room that will save me steps, but I see no desk for the writer of the house.

Dillard (1989) says this about locating a space to write: "Appealing workplaces are to be avoided. One wants a room with no view, so imagination can meet memory in the dark" (p. 26). I see her point, but I have just died and gone to window heaven. I could choose the long dining table with the view of the tiny beach below but it doesn't feel warm with its plastic table covering. I will eat my meals at one end of the table watching the sunset. Then get back to writing about my teaching. I choose the sitting area of the Gabriola Room. It's cozy. The overstuffed sofas and chair will keep my solitary self company as extended family, visitors. Yes, I have a plan.

I find a vintage TV tray, all the rage in the 1950s, with a veneer panel top, clipped on gold coloured aluminum legs crossing on either side. This will be my desk. The laptop fits on it with just enough room for the mouse. From the TV tray,

I will be facing the sea, and all that goes on in the fullness of a day. And I will be writing. Now, what about Dillard's advice?

The captain's chair from the dining room will do nicely for a desk chair with its tall straight back, worn velvet seat, and steady arms. I push the TV tray up against the windows with the Captain's chair facing the sea. How appropriate. The coffee table nearby serves as a side-desk for my writing accessories: notebooks, pencils and pens, printer and paper, books, speakers for listening to music, a stash of chocolate.

At night I will sit on the sofa near the wood stove with the laptop and wool blanket on my lap. Evening writing sessions require a fire, which requires wood, and the chore of splitting, stacking, starting the fire, and cleaning out the ashes from the stove. Eventually, this will inspire me to consider writing a poem called *Ode to a Thermostat!*

* * * *

The wall of windows frame a view of the Georgia Strait like a scenic painting would, saving forever the same distant panorama of the sea, islands, and the sky. In the foreground is a still life of trees silhouetted against water and sky, some with oddly curved trunks and branches, the up-close Arbutus has peeling copper bark. I will spend lots of time becoming familiar with this scene, seeing it as always the same, always there.

The wall of windows also holds the movement of the living sea. Its surface is alive, constantly forming intricate patterns, apparently at random. Who knows? Shimmers of light blink on and off. Whitecaps run with the wind, racing white fluffy clouds above to the horizon. From this perspective, I will become familiar with a changing scene, always there.

Today is my first day of writing. I sit in my Captain's chair at my tiny makeshift desk and watch the sun lead the day from east to west, painting the colours of the day. I become lost, from my Captain's chair, in the sun-drenched choppy waters, in the swift current, in the windswept sea of shimmering light. Later, I sit still and watch the moon rise and escort the night actors across the sky, a Greek hero, a Phoenician queen, a caravan of traveling zodiacs. Moon's long sparkling silver veil draped across the velvet black water comes through the windows and wraps me to my Captain's chair. My eyes grow tired by this hour and struggle to witness the impromptu dance of moonlight, sea, and wind still in full swing. I finally surrender to the night and to dreamtime, musing in the very last second, "Am I already asleep, or woken up by the magic of windows?"

>When you step into a world for a closer look
>you risk a change of heart,
>being swept away into uncharted waters,
>behaving like an attentive lover
>who desires at once to know every hidden detail
>about a new beloved.

* * * *

I have never really known for certain where my life was headed, only where it stopped short. Short of taking a closer look at what goes on off the beaten path, or playing truant away from the permitted, the expected, the routine. What would truancy feel like? No permission or explanation required. No excuses.

Today I decide to leave the cottage, no explanation other than it's time to explore the tiny beach I see from the windows. I load my backpack with binoculars, a water bottle, my brown moleskin notebook and pencil, an apple and some chocolate. My truant self heads down the overgrown path behind the cottage toward the untended and weather-worn wood steps that lead to the beach. It's a step by step diversion from the writing I am supposed to be doing, from the Captain's chair where I am supposed to be sitting. A wrong turn, perhaps?

At the juncture before the steps, I notice the remains of animal rituals, left behind by river otters and raccoons. This sacred spot signals some sort of threshold before the steps to the beach. I watch my footing, careful where I step so as to avoid sacrificing the bottom of my shoe. I am trespassing into a world that rarely receives human visitors. The densely lush bank emits commanding ribbits, chirps, and low hisses. The Jurassic period comes to mind. Before heading down the steps, I pause and ask myself, "Where am I headed?"

The beach is about 50 metres long, framed in tall evergreens, Arbutus, and a few maples that will show their true colours in the autumn. The stratum of white crushed shells gleams. The movement of sea has sculpted the sandstone banks along the shoreline into surreal formations etched with holes the size of rocks long since gone. These structures are the impressions of ocean waves ready to break. I noticed from the windows that the depth of exposed beach depends on the tide, its cycle in moon time, or its 'time of the month' as my mother used to say to her daughters. It is low tide. I have lots of beach to explore.

The beach is adjacent to flourishing tide pools. Low tide means exposure. Exotic creatures seek invisibility in the refuge of potholes and crevices eroded in the rocks. Tiny crabs scurry around my feet to secure shelter under anything that gives cover. Plump purple starfish, in bundles of entangled arms, wait stoically in sheltered rock clefts.

I lean my hand on a boulder to balance myself. The sensation on my palm and fingers tells me not to look closer. The boulder is alive. I feel it. Green and purple anemones, aggregates of them, uniformly blanket these boulders close to the water's edge. They never leave their spot in the crowd. Where would they go? At low tide these carnivores pull in their tentacles, losing their innocent flower-like disguise.

Some of these tidal creatures have ended up on the beach. A wrong turn, perhaps? I see large orange jellyfish left for dead by the tide, looking like giant broken ostrich eggs. I watch my step. I do not move them. I do not intervene.

The imagination lives for attentiveness,
to play find and seek.

* * * *

Despite my original plan, there lurks a conspiracy in the wind, in the tide, among the giant beached kelp that look like long snakes. I feel like Eve. I am seduced straightaway. My curiosity held hostage by this tiny Eden and its accomplices. A tenderfoot urbanite like me is easy prey in the wild. I am lured into spending my days sitting on the tiny beach below the cottage watching all that goes on in the fullness of a day, alongside the beached logs that look like the bleached bones of seafaring wanderers that never left, never got away. I bite my apple.

My writing about teaching is on hold. The Captain's chair empty. I head to the beach first thing every morning with my moleskin notebook, taking field notes, writing things down. Being a learner.

I step into moon time and feel the pull of a new clock, of the tide. The beach waxes and wanes magically, keeping time with the moon. The waterline moves ever so slowly like the hands of a clock. The same beach but never the same. I learn about impermanence.

There are no other humans here at the beach to act human with, to speak with. Being human is about being with other humans, doing what 'they' do. At the beach, alone, I am silent and even stop my own incessant inner dialogue for periods of time. After a few weeks, I become invisible. Not self-conscious. Invisible but uncovered, exposed as human. A bit weird.

Animals come to the beach, doing what they do everyday. Birds see all from above. When I put seed in the feeder the birds flock over like they have been waiting for table service. Seals stalk me. Big eyes in round shiny heads duck under the water when they see my binoculars or camera pointed at them.

Yesterday a river otter walked across the log right behind me. I turned to see it head to the water, never looking back. Not even a nod. This afternoon I sat close to the shore while writing in my notebook. I hadn't looked up in a while. But, my brain alerted me there was something very close, much bigger than an otter. Not human. I looked up to see a buck with a full rack of antlers, walking gracefully between me and the water. Even when our eyes met, neither of us made a run for it.

I've adapted to a non-human world, or shall I say more than human world. I am present, as human, as trespasser. It is a choice. Pretences will not work.

> A closer look takes place in person,
> in flesh and blood,
> with eyes, ears, feet, fingers, tongue,
> to explore being-here.

* * * *

The beach was not always beautiful. There were grey dreary days, and stark lonely nights. High tides covered the stratum of crushed white shells. Full moon's low tides uncovered foul smells, bones, and picked-over crustaceans that attracted bothersome insects. Predators competed for food.

One day I saw a group of small birds, about a half dozen, dive-bombing a crow or raven. The large black bird dodged the attacks with quick manoeuvres. It was struggling to both fly and carry in its claws a small bird struggling to get free. It was not long before the small dive-bombers gave up and flew away from the predator. As the black bird passed over my head a flow of small delicate feathers trailed behind dancing in the air with effortless grace, falling with all the time in the world.

> Life and death follow one another
> but neither leads the way

* * * *

At the beach, I'm immersed in a non-human soundscape with languages and codes new to me, especially around birds. When a crow flies the air wisps across its flapping wings. Hummingbirds wings buzz like large insects and make me flinch. Kingfisher has a loud rattling cry that announces its territory, "The king's back in town!" Stellar's Jay has an aggressive 'wah' call that scares away smaller birds at my feeder. Eagle has a high shrill sound that surprised me. I expected more bravado.

The most startling sound is the silence. It's never silent in the dense urban neighbourhood where I live. Here I attune my ear to the subtleties of movement—leaves, air, wings, water, footsteps, breath.

In the long days of late spring, life goes on as usual for these animals. They live here. Spring is an active time of year. Lots of gestations going on. The Strait is a fishing spot for birds and mammals, including rare visits by grey whales bottom feeding near the shore. Above all, afternoon soaring over the islands is popular among eagles and vultures. I am the quiet visitor grounded below looking up with oversized binoculars.

Inquiry takes time. It's a timeout, a truancy from the time clock that alarms me about how I ought to spend my time, day in, day out. Who can live like there's no tomorrow? Who has the time to sit and watch a day go by? It appears terribly unproductive. As did I. Nevertheless, there I sat in my low fold-up chair every day. The act of sitting and observing in one place, even on a tiny beach for a string of days, allowed me to see what goes on in the daily life of a place, a tiny beach. The question is not how can such a small event matter in the overall scheme of things in my life, but how can it influence how I see the world as a whole. I come closer to no tomorrow every moment but forget to take a look.

> Inquiry is an intimate experience.

* * * *

I have come to know animals that live at the beach. My favourite companion is a seagull I name Jonathan Livingston. JL hangs out with me most days, standing nearby on the rocks, or paddling back and forth in shallow water close to shore, turning his head from time to time to look at me. I smile back. In the air JL is an agile sprinter, and an ace at aerial sweeps of the beach. JL can hover, dive and climb quickly. His wings are built for manoeuvring, with a bend along the length and tips that point down, with the ability to morph into the exact shape that is most efficient for the task at hand.

JL seems different from urban seagulls, the ones that hang out in gangs and steel food from beach picnics. One day I see JL consume a starfish, arms sticking out from his beak in all directions. The victim takes time to digest, disappearing completely only after lots of up and down contortions of JL's head and neck. No chewing, just swallowing. This is about getting a star shape down a round hole. Afterwards, JL drops a starfish near where I am sitting. I graciously decline.

Adiós Gaviota!

* * * *

I sit at my kitchen table back in the city reading through my notebook, drinking tea. It is weathered, having been opened and closed so many times on the beach. The notebook documents a faithful account of my life there. I wrote things down. As I open the cover I remember the tiny bugs that came out of nowhere on the beach and scuttled across the curves of my handwriting as I wrote on an open page. Tiny spiders rappelled from the Arbutus trees with silk threads, touching down on a notebook page like a swat team, quickly checking out this landing pad, a shock to all of us. I would then spend the next five minutes evacuating them off my notebook safely to the sand, a difficult task with such fragile creatures. I laugh as I recall how they never once cooperated.

I never wrote those stories about my teaching. I did write about what matters to a teacher's life—notes about living like there was no tomorrow, about watching a day go by. The notes sketch a story of me stepping inside the world of a tiny beach, taking a closer look at what goes on off a beaten path, crossing a threshold of the more than human world. The beach was the teacher, irreducible and mystical, yet concrete and tangible like the sand under my fingernails or the seafaring trinkets I kept in my jacket pockets. The teachings offered me, a teacher of many years, another way to live and learn.

The days did not always pass pleasantly. I encountered dark times when loneliness gripped my heart, refusing to let go. But other times solitude rendered an immense joy in every fibre of my being. The heartache of loneliness and the joy of solitude both found a place in my life on the island. This human capacity to know both so deeply strikes me as extraordinary.

The ritual of packing up and loading the car went way too fast even though I tried to savour my back and forth trips, arms full. I noticed that the cord of wood under the blue tarp was half gone. Nothing like the sound of a successful split! I had made a list of my belongings from memory, the things I cannot do without, on a clean sheet of notebook paper so I would not leave anything behind. It sat on the TV tray until everything was packed in the car. My mind drifted between leaving the cottage and my memories of packing up to leave my grandparent's cabin. On the way home in the old Ford, the three of us kids always fell asleep in the backseat. My grandfather carried us to our beds. When I woke up I was home, already jumping ahead and imagining the next time at the cabin, that restless child. I never thought there would be a last time.

I stand on the deck, where Sally turned to wave at the camera, looking at the beach for a minute or two—brimmed hat, keys in one hand, notebook in the other. As I drive to the ferry I remind myself that life happens in the meanwhiles, between the fragments of stories. Still, the child in me jumps ahead, wondering when I will be back.

Life is a beach after all.

* * * *

REFERENCES

Dillard, A. (1989). *The writing life*. New York: HarperPerennial.

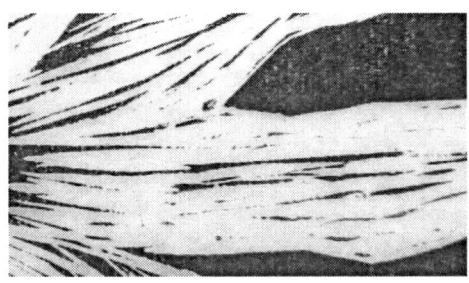

AVRAHAM COHEN

HAVING SPOKEN OF TEACHING

Life, Death, Pedagogy, and the Fine Art of Being Human

In order to rule the nation, you had best have able men, Naoshige said. Whereupon his son asked, Do you mean I have to pray to Buddha and the gods for the appearance of these men?

The father replied, After all you pray to God for things beyond human power and endeavor. It is within our power to get talented people to appear.

How then is it possible? He asked again.

Naoshige answered, Irrespective of any matter, things gather around him who loves them. If he loves flowers, every variety of flowers will begin to gather together about him, even though he has not had a single seed until that time. And, in due course, there will grow a flower of the rarest kind. Likewise, if you love people, the result will be the same. Make a point of loving and respecting. (Stone, 2001, pp. 40-41)

I believe that the content of the dialogue between Naoshige and his father applies well to the 'way of being' of exceptional teachers. They are known by the love and respect they have for their students, and for the consequent 'gathering around' and 'growing of the rarest kind.' Really, I think we are talking about their ability to connect with students. Such teachers convey their love and respect in diverse ways; never the same way twice—always consistent with circumstances and the student. I would count our group of professors who have authored this text to be amongst this group of teachers. There are, however, many excellent teachers outside the university, and outside any schools. Aunt Evalyn was one of them, and my dedication for this book bears her name.

As I write this, I am aware that Aunt Evalyn's funeral was just four days ago (August 15, 2011). My previous contact with her was at her 100th birthday party. Evalyn Kantor was not my biological aunt but she and her husband, Morrie, became close friends to my parents, and as it turned out she became an important person in my life. Her pleasure at seeing me at her 100th birthday was palpable and reminded me of the good feelings I always had in her presence from my earliest memories of her, which go back to when I was six years old. My memories about her and my relationship with her are mostly in the feeling dimension. When I was in her presence as a child I always felt that I was good, and a similarly as an adult I always felt whole. As I reflect now I would say that she represented the core of what makes a great teacher: a steadfast presence of kindness, warmth, encouragement, nurturance, an ability to see clearly and articulate in the moment, and most of all, aliveness. As well, great teachers are resourceful, present in the moment, capable of thinking on their feet, and perhaps a most telling hallmark of a great teacher is that they are still with you even years later and even after they no longer walk on the earth in a physical form.

What is arising in my consciousness as I reflect on the writings in our book is the well-known, and in my view often misunderstood statement, 'When the student is ready the teacher will appear.' Teachers don't appear at some specific moments: they are everywhere all the time in both the animate and inanimate world. Some of them will show up for a second, some for a few moments, and some for much longer. Clearly, some teachers have more impact on students, and on more students than others. Great teachers, in my view, are those who will create conditions that predispose students to be increasingly alert to their own learning moments and learning possibilities. They seem to create these conditions with their ability to be fully present, the ability to be responsive to what arises in the moment, with their consummate subject knowledge, and with their in-the-moment passion that transcends content and skills. All essays in this book reveal something about what makes for excellent teachers. Certainly, their presence and their work here have had and continue to have a significant impact on me.

In closing, I wish to share with you a brief fragment from each of my colleagues along with some reflections in response to their thoughts:

Marion: ". . . recognizing ourselves as teachers who are influential."

Marion's comment reminds me of my own, at times, genuine surprise and occasional trepidation that go along with the realization that students are remembering my words, taking me seriously, and are influenced by me. Perhaps surprise and trepidation are the 'right' feelings to have in the service of proper use of power and influence. Recognizing that we are doing something, and that what we do, and how we do something is an essential ingredient of self-awareness and a chief ingredient of learning and transformation. Sensitivity and awareness to the influence and effect teachers have on students' learning and state of being is central to a teacher's work. Students do notice and respond to the influence and power that teachers hold. As educators, I believe we cannot escape having this power and influence. However, we can be aware of it and honour it, and with this awareness and a well-developed ethical sense use it judiciously and wisely.

Tony: "The invitation to meet as a group was an opportunity to enjoy each other's company, something that did not happen often in our professional lives."

Tony's comment shines light on the relative paucity of direct attention to the human and social dimension in academic environments. The ethos of busy-ness and business prevails in academic environments. Colleagues who have worked nearby each other for decades often do not know each other as persons in any substantial way, and when they move on or retire the most frequent occurrence is an almost instantaneous diminishing or total lack of contact. Our group seems to demonstrate that personal knowing of colleagues and community building can be the foundation for both the business and personal side of the academy. I would say that, in our case, the attention to the subjective and intersubjective realms has been the vital energy that has nurtured our creativity, production, and sense of connection. I believe that these elements are synergistically connected.

Heesoon: "Where does this inability to be in the here-and-now come from?"

Heesoon reminds me of what I often see as the symptom of and immense problem in educational environments: dullness and dispiritedness. So often what is seen as learning is not of current or real relevance to students. I believe that teachers who are initiators and progenitors of such an environment are not sufficiently engaged emotionally, physically, intuitively or even intellectually. In short, they are not present in a meaningful and substantial way. Cultivation of the ability to be fully present is in the service of cultivating the ability to connect with and engage students. Of course, such cultivation requires deep and ongoing inner work that identifies and works to transform that which intervenes and prevents full presence.

Karen: "Every person has gifts. My job is to help those gifts to emerge."

For me, this statement defines a central aspect of being a teacher: Recognition that everyone has gifts to offer to the world, facilitating conditions for those offerings to emerge, and an absence of need to be the centre of attention. I had the good fortune of being a student in Karen's class and witnessed first hand her way of being in a classroom. There were moments when she would offer her own experience in a way that showed us something about her and also demonstrated a pedagogical point. She made it clear, by example, that it was quite fine to include ourselves as part of the subject of learning and that there are ways to do this that make it engaging and pedagogically significant for those who are in the learner's position.

Carl: "I have been in school since I was four years old . . . For more than a half century I have been connected with schools."

Any profession or trade belongs in a personal way to those who love the work they do, and who are in the 'right' work. I believe that Carl speaks here as a person who has been in the right place at the right time, knows it, and is sufficiently alert that he does not disrupt the flow of life as it unfolds in harmony with himself and the universe. This seems to me to epitomize what makes a great teacher. As Carl states in his essay, he has given his heart to being an educator. Teaching, I believe, is a devotional act.

On behalf of our group I wish to express our sincere hope that the seeds of your devotion will also grow and bear fruit.

In the beginning there is no beginning,
In the end there is no end.

REFERENCES

Stone, J. F. (Ed.). (2001). *Bushido: The way of the samurai* (Based on the Hagakure by Tsunetomo Yamamoto) (M. Tanaka, Trans.). Garden City Park, NY: Square One.

ABOUT THE AUTHORS OF SPEAKING OF TEACHING

Avraham Cohen: What matters *is* what matters. I have spent my life so far following the guiding star of what matters and using my digressions from the pathway as learning moments. I propose that the initiator of humane environments in education is the teacher, the educational leader, who if not a sage, is alive to the possibilities of living within the process of becoming so. . . and, I have published a lot, read a lot, and talked a lot to others about what matters.

* * *

Marion Porath: As an educator, I construct, compose, sense, represent, celebrate intricacy and complexity, colour my world, notice, unite perspectives, ponder, polish. Artistry brings me closer to the heart of pedagogy.

* * *

Anthony Clarke: Tony, you are often regarded as diligent and organized . . . err, sorry, what was that? Your Mum is calling you? For dinner? But it is only 3.30 in the afternoon. And, doesn't your Mum live in Australia? Oh, she has a loud voice. Lamb stew. And roast potatoes. It does sounds nice. Ahhhh, what about the bio for the book? Any words of wisdom? Oh really. And that helps? OK. Do a cartwheel before going to bed. It's probably not what they were expecting.

***

Heesoon Bai: I am in recovery: of my humanity, sanity, animism, kairos, zen, original face, primordial confidence, ceaseless and immeasurable compassion, nameless wisdom, and most of all, boundless love. I spent the first half of my life in surviving and succeeding, and now, I wish to dedicate the second half to unlearning, undoing, unbinding, and unleashing—in short, to remedial education.

* * *

Carl Leggo: As an educator, I am Aokian, Baktinian, Cixousian, Deweyan, Eisnerian, Freirean, Girouxian, Huebnerian, Illichian, Jungian, Kohlian, Latherian, Marxian, Noddingsian, O'Sullivanian, Postmanian, Quindlenian, Russellian, Seussian, Tompkinsian, Underhillian, Vanierian, Whiteheadian, Xavierian, Youngian, Zizekian. I am still not sure who I am, but I am alive, happy, and in love, always in love.

* * *

ABOUT THE AUTHORS

Karen Meyer: I want nothing more than to be a good writer, teacher, drummer, partner, mother, grandmother, daughter, and friend. The epitaph can later read: "Karen had a good life. She was an upstanding character with wobbly legs."

* * *

CPSIA information can be obtained at www.ICGtesting.com
Printed in the USA
LVOW081927041012

301550LV00002B/1/P